BADMINTON

Sixth Edition

DATE DUE

About the Authors

Margaret Varner Bloss's experience is confined neither to her native Texas nor to the United States but spreads throughout the world.

She is the only person ever to represent the United States in international competition in three racket sports: tennis (Wightman Cup), squash rackets (Wolfe-Noel Cup), and badminton (Uber Cup).

In addition to being the National Junior Girls' Doubles Tennis Champion, Mrs. Bloss was a member of the United States Wightman Cup Team in 1961 and 1962 and coach and/or captain of that team 1963–66. She holds United States and All-England titles in badminton: world champion 1955 and 1956; mixed doubles champion 1960; four years as world invitation ladies' doubles champion, Glasgow, Scotland. In 1969 she was captain of the U.S. Uber Cup Team. In squash rackets: National ladies' singles champion in 1960–63; U.S. mixed doubles champion in 1961; and member of the U.S. Wolfe-Noel Team in 1959 and 1963, and of the Philadelphia Howe Cup Team 1959–63.

Mrs. Bloss is also known for her books and articles on badminton and other sports. She has conducted workshops and clinics on tennis and badminton at Wellesley College, and the universities of Maryland, Delaware, Utah, and Texas Woman's. She has traveled throughout the world giving talks, exhibitions, and clinics.

Mrs. Bloss lives with her son in El Paso, Texas, where she continues her interest in sports and, with Margaret Osborne duPont, breeds and raises race-horses.

In 1985, R. Stanton (Stan) Hales became President of the United States Badminton Association for a three-year term after a 30-year career as badminton player, coach, and administrator.

He was the United States Junior Boys' Singles and Doubles Champion in 1959 and 1960, and was also Junior Mixed Doubles Champion in 1960. He later won the U.S. Men's Singles title twice, in 1970 and 1971; and in 1972 he advanced to the round of 16 in the All-England Championships. He represented the United States in Thomas Cup competition in 1967 and 1970, and he was the coach of the U.S. Thomas Cup team in 1976. He has served as a Director of the U.S.B.A. for over fifteen years. In 1985, he became the first American to be certified as an international umpire by the International Badminton Federation.

Dr. Hales holds a Ph.D. in mathematics from Harvard University. He is Professor of Mathematics and Associate Dean of the College at Pomona College, where he coaches the intercollegiate badminton team.

Dr. Hales lives in Claremont, California, with his wife Diane, who is a former Uber Cup player, a former national champion in singles and doubles, and a badminton coach. Their children Karen and Christopher are both badminton competitors.

BADMINTON
Sixth Edition

Margaret Varner Bloss
Former World Badminton Champion

R. Stanton Hales
Pomona College

 Wm. C. Brown Publishers

Book Team

Editor *Chris Rogers*
Developmental Editor *Cindy Kuhrasch*
Production Coordinator *Kay Driscoll*

 Wm. C. Brown Publishers

President *G. Franklin Lewis*
Vice President, Publisher *George Wm. Bergquist*
Vice President, Publisher *Thomas E. Doran*
Vice President, Operations and Production *Beverly Kolz*
National Sales Manager *Virginia S. Moffat*
Advertising Manager *Ann M. Knepper*
Marketing Manager *Kathy Law Laube*
Production Editorial Manager *Colleen A. Yonda*
Production Editorial Manager *Julie A. Kennedy*
Publishing Services Manager *Karen J. Slaght*
Manager of Visuals and Design *Faye M. Schilling*

Consulting Editor
Physical Education
Aileene Lockhart
Texas Women's Univeristy

Sports and Fitness Series
Evaluation Materials Editor
Jane A. Mott
Texas Women's University

Cover design by Jeanne Marie Regan

Cover photo by Mad City Tech

Library of Congress Catalog Card Number: 89–60198

ISBN 0–697–10390–0

Printed in the United States of America by Wm. C. Brown Publishers,
2460 Kerper Boulevard, Dubuque, IA 52001

10   9   8   7   6   5   4   3   2

Contents

Preface

This book is designed for all players who wish to learn or improve their badminton game; the information presented is suitable for and useful to players at all levels: backyard, club, or tournament. The book provides an organized description of how best to play and enjoy the game. Beginning students can learn the essentials by following the step-by-step instructions in the text. Advanced students can refresh forgotten techniques by skimming the table of contents and paragraph headings to locate particular material.

Every student of badminton must learn not only *how* to execute fundamental techniques but also *when* and *why* they should be used. These issues are addressed by the instructions, analyses, drills, and self-evaluation questions in the text. Also included are sections on equipment and tournament play, a bibliography of the growing literature on badminton, and a glossary.

Enhancing the text are both the precision of line drawings and the realism of selected photographs. The artist has made it possible for badminton students to learn from the drawings the subtle muscle changes that occur in various arm and body movements. In one sense, the drawings are as realistic as the photographs because of this precision. On the other hand, carefully chosen photographs alone can show the power and grace achieved by current top players.

The combination of the clear text, precise illustrations, dramatic photographs, and updated material throughout will enable badminton enthusiasts to increase their enjoyment of the game.

Introduction

1

Badminton is a game played with rackets on a court divided by a net. It is distinguished from other racket sports, all of which use a ball of some size, by two intriguing features: the use of a shuttlecock and the fact that the shuttlecock must not touch the ground during a rally. The flight characteristics of the shuttlecock and the pace created by constant volleying combine to make badminton one of the most exciting sports to play and to watch.

Historical Notes

Badminton has a long and fascinating history. With roots in China over two thousand years ago, it was purely recreational until a competitive version was developed in India and England in the mid- and late-nineteenth century. Since that time, the game has gained tremendous popularity in many countries. It is a major sport in most countries of northern Europe and Southeast Asia and is considered virtually the national sport in Indonesia and several other countries. Denmark, England, Sweden, and West Germany lead the European nations in their interest. The game spread in the 1870s to Canada and the United States, where national organizations similar to those of other countries were formed in the 1930s. Chapter 8 contains a fuller history of the game.

Badminton for Fitness and Recreation

As leisure time increases, badminton will no doubt play a more important role in the fitness and recreational programs so vital to the American citizen. It can be played by men, women, and children of all ages with a minimum of expense and effort. The game itself is stimulating mentally and physically, and it combines the values of individual and team sports. The fact that it can be learned easily makes it enjoyable from the outset. Basic techniques are easy to learn, yet much practice and concentration are required to perfect the skills needed for becoming an excellent badminton player.

Badminton in the World

Badminton took a giant step in 1985 when it was admitted to the Olympic Games as a full-medal sport starting in 1992. The International Badminton Federation, which already consisted of approximately 85 member nations at the time, will no doubt grow to nearly 150 nations by the first Olympic competition. Primarily an amateur sport until 1980, badminton now offers a world Grand Prix circuit for the top players, as well as a year-round season of tournaments and international competitions. Badminton is well on its way towards becoming a major world sport.

The Game

Badminton can be played indoors or outdoors, under artificial or natural lighting. Because of the wind, however, all tournament play is indoors. There may be one player on a side (the singles game) or two players on a side (the doubles game). The shuttlecock does not bounce; it is played in the air, making for an exceptionally fast game requiring quick reflexes and superb conditioning. There is a wide variety of strokes in the game ranging from powerfully hit smashes (over 150 mph!) to very delicately played dropshots.

Badminton is great fun because it is easy to learn—the racket is light and the shuttlecock can be hit back and forth (rallies) even when the players possess a minimum of skill. Within a week or two after the beginning of a class, rallies and scoring can take place. There are very few sports in which it is possible to get the feeling of having become an "instant player." However, do not assume that perfection of strokes and tournament caliber of play is by any means less difficult in badminton than in other sports.

A typical rally in badminton singles consists of a serve and repeated high deep shots hit to the baseline (clears), interspersed with dropshots. If and when a short clear or other type of "set-up" is forced, a smash wins the point. More often than not, an error (shuttle hit out-of-bounds or into the net) occurs rather than a positive playing finish to the rally. A player with increasing skill should commit fewer errors and make more outright winning plays to gain points. A player who is patient and commits few or no outright errors often wins despite not being as naturally talented as the opponent, by simply waiting for the opponent to err.

In doubles, there are fewer clears and more low serves, drives, and net play. (All of these terms are described in the following text.) Again, the smash often terminates the point. As in singles, patience and the lack of unforced errors are most desirable. Team play and strategy in doubles are very important, and often two players who have perfected their doubles system (rotating up and back on offense and defense) and choice of shots can prevail over two superior stroke players lacking in sound doubles teamwork and strategy.

Scoring

A badminton game consists of 15 points, except for women's singles in which a game is 11 points. The best of three games constitutes a match. Points can be scored only by the serving side. The sides change ends at the beginning of the second game and at the beginning of the third if a third game is necessary. In a 15-point game, ends are changed in the third game when the leading side reaches 8; in an 11-point game ends are changed when either side reaches 6. The side that wins a game serves first in the next game.

Unlike table tennis, a game does not need to be won when a player leads by 2 points. If the score becomes tied near the end of a game, the game may be lengthened by a procedure called "setting," described in chapter 2—Rules of Play, which also describes the serving rotation in singles and doubles, the various faults during play, and instructions for officiating.

Equipment for Badminton

To play the game of badminton, you need a court with a net, a racket, and a shuttlecock. The Laws of Badminton (see Appendix) contain formal requirements for this equipment. The most important of these specifications are presented in the discussions below.

The Court

Measurements of the singles and doubles playing courts are shown in figures 1.1 and 1.2. The singles court is 17 ft. wide and 44 ft. long; the doubles court is 3 feet wider because of the two side alleys. There are also a center line, a short service line, and a doubles long service line.

The court is bisected laterally by a net elevated five feet (5') above the ground at the center of the court and five feet one inch (5'1") at the net posts, which are placed on the doubles sidelines. When the game is played indoors, usually on a gymnasium floor, the ceiling should be not less than thirty feet (30') over the full-court area, and this space should be entirely free of girders and other obstructions. There should be at least four feet (4') of clear floor space surrounding each court and between any two courts.

The lines of the court should be white or yellow, and they must be 1½ inches wide. Unfortunately, many school gymnasium floors in the United States have badminton lines only 1 inch wide. These should be corrected eventually, and new courts should abide by the Laws.

An appropriate layout of courts in a gymnasium is shown in figure 1.3.

Rackets

For many years, rackets were made entirely of wood. Shafts made of steel or fiberglass were introduced in the 1950s, but a revolution in materials technology has made wood rackets obsolete. Virtually all rackets of quality are now constructed of various blends of steel, aluminum, carbon, graphite, and boron. These

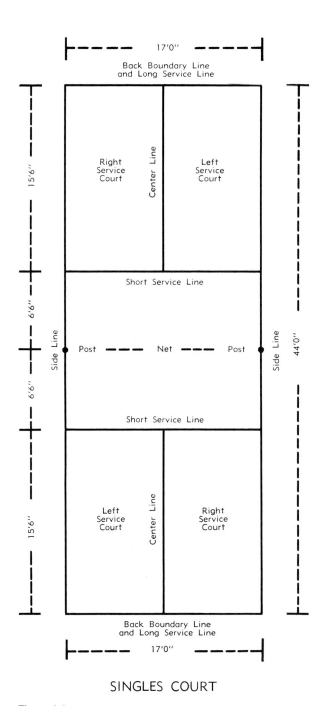

SINGLES COURT

Figure 1.1
Singles court.

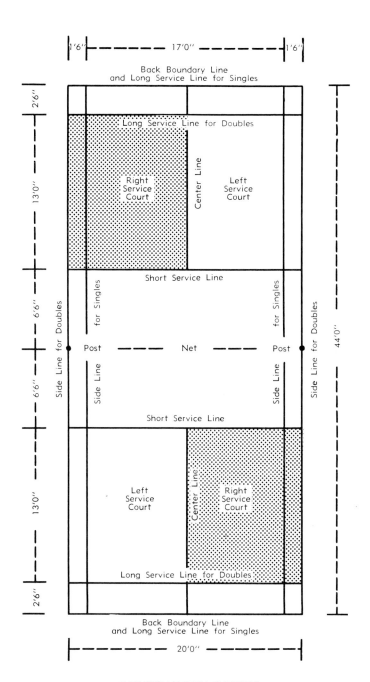

COMBINATION COURT

Figure 1.2
Combination court for singles and doubles.

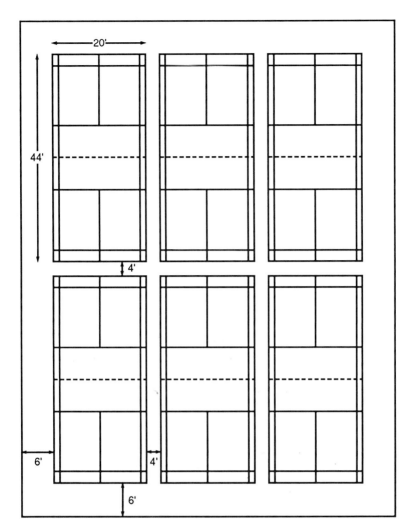

Figure 1.3
Court layout in gymnasium.

rackets are very light—around 3.5 ounces—and so strong that they can be strung much tighter than before. Also, the modern rackets do not warp and hence need no press. The racket's overall dimensions cannot exceed 27 inches by 9 inches, and the length of the head cannot exceed 11½ inches (fig. 1.4).

Each racket manufacturer offers several models to suit each player's ability to play and pay; prices vary from $10 to $120. Since the racket is the most important item of equipment, novices should ask a more-experienced player to help them to select one. The cheaper rackets are heavier, and hence often more durable, but not so easy to swing quickly. The more expensive rackets are lighter and more flexible, but can suffer damage more easily in collisions with the floor or a partner's racket. Some experimenting is suggested before one chooses a racket to buy.

Figure 1.4
Rackets and shuttlecocks.

The better known brands of rackets are Adidas, Black Knight, Carlton, Dunlop, HL, I.S.I., Kawasaki, Pro-Kennex, Slazenger, Sportcraft, Sugiyama, Vicourt, Victor, Yamaha, and Yonex. Few sporting goods stores in the United States carry a full line of rackets, although most will handle special orders in large quantities. It is often easier to order through dealers in badminton supplies; see chapter 9.

Rackets are strung with gut or some sort of synthetic string, like nylon. In the past, better players preferred gut, but the synthetics now equal the popularity of gut because the racket can be strung more tightly with them and because the synthetics cost less and last longer. A racket should be strung at between 15 and 20 lbs. tension, and a racket cover is suggested to protect the strings.

Rackets normally come with a handle grip made of leather. Replacement grips are available in leather, gauze, and towel.

Shuttlecocks

The traditional feathered shuttlecock is used in all major competitions. Various synthetic shuttles are acceptable, and especially suitable for club and school play, if their flight characteristics are similar. The feathered shuttle must weigh from 4.74–5.50 grams and have fourteen to sixteen feathers fixed in a cork base covered with a thin layer of leather or similar material. The required dimensions of the shuttle are given in the Laws—see Appendix. These requirements give the shuttle its unusual, although predictable, flight patterns.

In synthetic shuttles, the feathers are replaced by a "skirt" of some manufactured material, but such shuttles must meet the specifications of the feather shuttle. A good synthetic shuttle costs slightly less than the feather shuttle and normally lasts longer.

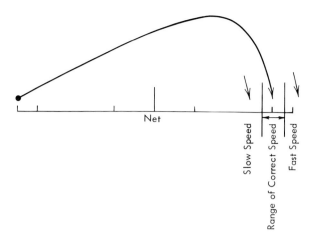

Figure 1.5
Shuttle test.

Bruce Hazelton / Focus West

Both kinds of shuttles, but especially the feather shuttles, will last much longer if they are humidified. This keeps the shuttle from drying, becoming brittle, and thus breaking. This is simple to do: glue a small piece of sponge on the inside of the cap of the tube which holds the shuttles, and keep the sponge damp.

In order to insure the game's taking the same form whenever and wherever it is played, it is imperative to standardize a shuttle's speed. A profound difference in the type of game results if a fast shuttle instead of a slow shuttle is selected for use. The heavier the shuttle, the faster it flies. Each grain adds about four inches in length to its flight. The shuttle also flies faster under conditions of increased temperature and altitude. Weights of manufactured shuttles therefore vary from 73 to 85 grains in order to meet conditions at a particular time; some manufacturers merely classify shuttles as slow, medium, or fast. Under normal conditions, a 78- to 80-grain (medium) shuttle is appropriate. Each time the game is played, the shuttle should function at the same speed regardless of atmospheric conditions.

In order to insure the game's taking the same form whenever and wherever it is played, it is imperative to standardize a shuttle's speed. A profound difference in the type of game results if a fast shuttle instead of a slow shuttle is selected for use. The heavier the shuttle, the faster it flies. The shuttle also flies faster under conditions of increased temperature and altitude. Weights of manufactured shuttles therefore vary in order to meet conditions at a particular time; some manufacturers merely classify shuttles as slow, medium, or fast. Under normal conditions, a medium (5.1 gram) shuttle is appropriate. Each time the game is played, the shuttle should function at the same speed regardless of atmospheric conditions. The speed of the shuttle can be altered by crimping the stalks of the feathers near the tip and bending them slightly—outward to slow the shuttle and inward to speed it up.

The testing of a shuttle's speed takes place at the beginning of a match. The test is made by having a player strike the shuttle with a full underhand stroke from a spot directly above one back boundary line in a direction parallel to the sideline and at an upward angle. It must land in a three-foot range centered on the opposite doubles long service line (fig. 1.5).

The better known brands of feather shuttles are Black Knight, Flying, HL, Rackets International, RSL, Sportcraft, Victor, and Yonex. The price for a tube of a dozen varies from $15 to $20. Synthetic shuttles are manufactured by most of these companies, as well as by Carlton, EST International, Thunderbird, Wilson, and others. Some synthetic shuttles are available in yellow for better visibility in halls with light-colored walls. It is important to buy better quality synthetics, which cost about $12 per dozen, because the cheaper ones seldom have correct speed or satisfactory flight characteristics.

Rules of Play

2

The International Badminton Federation annually publishes a Statute Book containing the Laws of Badminton as well as interpretations and revisions of the laws. The United States Badminton Association adopts these laws for badminton play in this country, and it also publishes a Handbook containing them. The Laws of Badminton are reproduced in full in the Appendix, as they existed at time of publication. Because the laws change from time to time, a current official handbook should be consulted for any tournament play. However, the summary in this chapter of the rules of play will suffice for school, college, and recreational badminton. The rules on playing equipment are summarized in chapter 1.

Summary of the Laws

Players

1. Players are those persons taking part in the game: one player on a side in singles, two players on a side in doubles. The side which has the serve is called the "in" side and the opposing side, the "out" side.

Toss

2. Before play begins, the opposing sides shall toss a coin or a racket. The winner of the toss shall have the option of serving first, not serving first, or choosing ends of the court. The side losing the toss shall then have a choice of the remaining alternatives. Decisions made at this time can be very important. One end of the court may be more desirable than the other because of lighting arrangements, floor conditions, and location of spectators.

Serving and Scoring

3. Play is started by an underhand serve and a side can score only when serving (fig. 2.3). Each time an exchange or rally is won while serving, one point is recorded. If the rally is lost while serving, neither side is awarded a point. Instead, the right to serve is relinquished and the serve passes to the opponent (in singles) or the next player in rotation (doubles).

4. Doubles and men's singles games consists of 15 points; women's singles, 11 points. Peculiar to the scoring system is the term "setting." This is a method of extending the length of a game if the game is tied at a particular score. For example, when the score becomes tied at "13-all" in a 15-point game, the side which reached 13 first has the option of "setting" the game to 5 (a total of 18 points), so that the side that scores 5 points first wins the game. The score may be set in the same manner at "14-all" for 3 points (a total of 17 points). In women's singles, the 11-point game may total 12 points by setting at "9-all" for 3 points or "10-all" for 2 points. See the chart below.

Points in Game	Score Tied at	Game May Be Set To
11	9 all	3 points
11	10 all	2 points
15	13 all	5 points
15	14 all	3 points

The side which reached the tied score first has the option of setting or not setting the score. If the side elects not to set the score, then the conventional number of points completes the game. If a side does not set the score at the first opportunity, either side may have the opportunity, however, to set the score should the occasion arise again. In doubles, for example, if the score is tied at 13-all, and the team that reached 13 first declared no set, then play continues to 15. If, then, the score becomes tied at 14-all, whichever team reached 14 first is offered the opportunity to set the score. The score of a match could thus be 15–14, 16–18, 17–16.

5. A match shall consist of the best of three games. The players change ends at the beginning of the second game and at the beginning of the third game, if a third game is necessary to decide the match. In the third game, players shall change ends when either player first reaches 8 in a game of 15 points and 6 in a game of 11 points. The object of this change of ends is to try to give both players equal time on both ends of the court. If players forget to change ends, they shall change as soon as their mistake is discovered.

6. An *inning* is a term of service and there may be any number of innings since many rallies are played for which no points are scored.

7. A serve is deemed completed as soon as the shuttle is struck by the server's racket. Unlike the serve in tennis, only one serve is allowed a player to put the shuttle into play.

8. A shot falling inside the boundaries or directly on a line is considered good.

9. When any unusual occurrence interferes with the play, a "let" (replay of the point) can be invoked. This happens, for example, if a stray shuttle from a nearby court interferes, or if a linesman and umpire are unable to make a decision on a particular shot.

When the score is tied at 13-all, which team has the option of setting? If the team elects not to set and the score then becomes tied at 14-all, what happens?

Serving Rotation

10. *Singles* In singles, the players serve from and receive in the right service court when the server's score is an even number. When the server's score is an odd number, the players serve from and receive in the left service court. See figure 2.1 for a typical serving sequence.

11. *Doubles* In doubles, the service rotation is determined by the score and by positions on the court at the start of the game. In this way, badminton is different from other racket sports in which the rotation is fixed. Figure 2.2 illustrates this process in a typical serving sequence. The side serving first in a game has only one turn at serve. The server delivers the first serve from the right service court to the receiver in the right service court on the opposing side and then alternates service courts as long as rallies are won. The

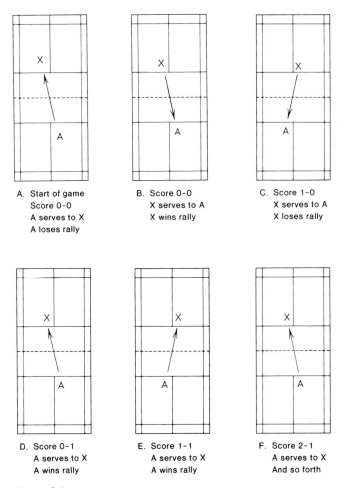

A. Start of game
Score 0-0
A serves to X
A loses rally

B. Score 0-0
X serves to A
X wins rally

C. Score 1-0
X serves to A
X loses rally

D. Score 0-1
A serves to X
A wins rally

E. Score 1-1
A serves to X
A wins rally

F. Score 2-1
A serves to X
And so forth

Figure 2.1
Typical singles serving sequence.

receiving side does not change courts. After this first inning, *both* players on a side have a turn at serve before the serve passes to the other side. In each successive inning, the "first server" is the player who by the team's score is correctly in the right service court when his or her team regains the serve. The first server serves until a rally is lost; and then the serve passes to the "second server," without courts being changed. The second server continues to serve, alternating courts, until a rally is lost, and then the serve goes over to the other side.

Thus, when the serving side's score is an even number, the server should be standing in the service court (right or left) in which he or she began the game. When the side's score is an odd number, the server should be in the opposite service court. The same applies to the receiver and the receiving

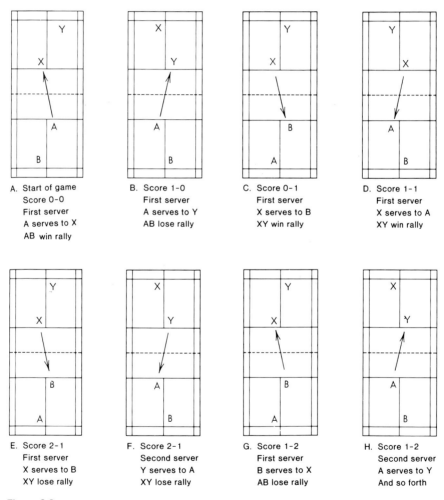

A. Start of game
   Score 0-0
   First server
   A serves to X
   AB win rally

B. Score 1-0
   First server
   A serves to Y
   AB lose rally

C. Score 0-1
   First server
   X serves to B
   XY win rally

D. Score 1-1
   First server
   X serves to A
   XY win rally

E. Score 2-1
   First server
   X serves to B
   XY lose rally

F. Score 2-1
   Second server
   Y serves to A
   XY lose rally

G. Score 1-2
   First server
   B serves to X
   AB lose rally

H. Score 1-2
   Second server
   A serves to Y
   And so forth

Figure 2.2
Typical doubles serving sequence.

side's score. During the serve, the partners of the server and receiver may stand anywhere on the court. After the serve is delivered, players on both sides may take any positions on the court they wish.

The score in a singles match is 8 for player A and 5 for player B who is serving. From which court should B serve next?

Faults

The Laws of Badminton include certain points that cannot be violated without penalty. If any violation of the following laws occurs, it is a fault on the offending side. If the receiving side faults, the serving side scores a point. If the serving side faults, no point is scored and the serve passes to the next appropriate server.

Faults During Serving and Receiving

12. A serve must be an underhand stroke and the entire shuttle must be below the server's waist on contact. To insure that the serve is an underhand stroke, the shaft of the racket must point downwards at the time of contact, to such an extent that the entire head of the racket is discernibly below the hand and fingers holding the racket (figs. 2.3 and App. fig. 5).
13. A player's feet must be stationary and in their correct court upon delivery of the serve. It is not a fault if a server takes up his stance and then takes one step forward, provided he has not started to swing his racket before completing the step.
14. The server should not serve until the receiver is ready. If the receiver attempts to return the serve, however, he is judged ready. If a player is not ready, he should let the shuttle fall to the court and then tell the server or the umpire that he was not ready, in which case the serve shall be delivered again. This rule keeps the player who has a tendency to hurry his opponent from gaining an undue advantage.

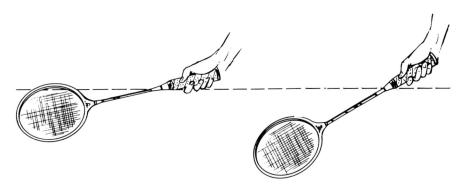

Figure 2.3
Illegal serve, legal serve.

15. Once the service has started, no preliminary feints or movements to distract the receiver are allowed. The first forward movement of the server's racket constitutes the start of the service. A preliminary feint is any movement by the server that has the effect of breaking the continuity of the serve after the two players have taken their ready positions to begin the point. Such action is termed a balk, and a balk is a fault. It is also a fault if the server delays hitting the shuttle for so long as to be unfair to the receiver.
16. If a player attempting a serve misses the shuttle completely, it is a fault.
17. A serve that lands outside the boundaries of the service court is a fault. See figure 1.2, chapter 1 for service court boundaries.
18. A player may not serve or receive out of turn or from the wrong court. The consequences of an infraction of this rule depend upon when the mistake is discovered. If the player who commits one of these serving or receiving errors wins the rally, and the mistake is then discovered, a let is called. If the player at fault loses the rally, the mistake stands, that is, no let. If the mistake is not discovered before the next point commences, the already altered serving and receiving order is not changed until the end of the game regardless of which team won or lost the rally.
19. The receiver's partner may not strike a serve meant for the receiver.

Faults During Play

20. If the shuttle falls outside the boundaries, passes through or under the net, fails to pass the net, touches the roof or side walls, or touches a person or the dress of a person, the rally ceases and the player committing the fault is penalized. However, a serve hitting the top of the net and going into the correct service court is legal and "in play." Some gymnasiums or halls may have low beams, ropes, or other obstructions hanging over the court. In such cases the local association may establish a ground rule to the effect that a shuttle hitting the obstruction would not be considered a fault, but a let. If careful judgment by an experienced person is not made in this case, a player might intentionally hit the obstruction when it appeared that he was going to lose the point. If an obstruction can be hit deliberately, the fault rule is usually enforced. An unusual and uncommon situation develops when a shuttle passes the net outside of the net post and then flies into the court. This is the only case in which the shuttle can go below the net level and still be legal.
21. A player may not reach over the net to contact a shuttle. He may, however, contact the shuttle on his side of the net and follow through with his racket on the opponent's side, providing the net is not touched.
22. When the shuttle is "in play" a player may not touch the net or the net posts with his body, his racket, or his clothing. If he should hit the net following a stroke and after his shot has struck the floor, a fault does not result because the shuttle is not "in play" after it strikes the floor.
23. The shuttle may not be hit twice in succession before being returned to the opponent. This rule prevents setting the shuttle up to oneself or to one's partner.

24. The shuttle may not be caught on the racket and then slung during the execution of the stroke. Commonly called "carry," "sling," or "throw," this fault is difficult to detect and it is often committed unintentionally by beginners because of poor timing. More advanced players seldom commit this fault outright, but occasionally when a deceptive technique is attempted the infraction may occur. When a "carry" is committed, the shuttle's speed and direction are changed. This naturally handicaps the receiver of such a shot, and a player should not be penalized by another player's poor technique. The rule, then, is an essential one, and any player at fault should immediately call "No Shot."

25. A fault is called when a player is hit by the shuttle whether he is standing inside or outside the court boundaries. It is surprising to many players to realize that if they are able to hit their opponent with the shuttle, the point is theirs! This, however, is more difficult to accomplish than it sounds.

26. If a shuttle is hit into the net or caught in the net on the striker's side, it is not "in play." If the shuttle goes over the net, but catches on the other side, a let results. The point is replayed since the player on whose side the shuttle was caught did not have a fair chance of returning the shuttle. If the player attempted to play the shuttle that was caught in the net and in doing so hit the net, then a "fault," rather than a let, would be called.

27. A player may not step on his opponent's side of the net even when, in returning a close net shot, he cannot stop his momentum until his feet are in his opponent's court.

28. A player may not intentionally hold his racket near the net, obstructing the opponent's stroke, hoping that the shuttle will happen to rebound from his racket into the opponent's court. This occasionally happens when a player close to the net tries to defend against a smash. On the other hand, a racket held in front of a player's face for protection is a good maneuver and any resulting shot is acceptable.

29. A player may not "unsight" another player during service. This rule, applicable only in doubles, means that the server's partner must not stand in front of the server in such a way that the receiver cannot see the shuttle about to be served. If this situation occurs, the receiver tells the server or the umpire, before the shuttle is served, that he cannot see the shuttle. An adjustment of the starting positions is then made by the serving side.

30. Play must be continuous. A player therefore may not leave the court, receive advice, or rest at any time from the start to the conclusion of the match except during the interval described below. The umpire shall judge whether this rule has been broken, and a player violating this rule may be warned, faulted, or disqualified. Most countries allow a five-minute rest period between the second and third games. In the United States a five-minute rest interval is allowed in all matches if any player requests it.

A thorough and accurate knowledge of the rules makes for smooth, pleasurable game. Many misunderstandings can be avoided by the player who knows not only the rules but the reasons for them.

Unwritten Rules

Badminton, like all sports, has unwritten as well as written rules. The common courtesies, or etiquette, of badminton commence with your first introduction to the game.

Conduct on the Court

During the warm up:

1. Agree on a correct shuttle for use.
2. Hit the shuttle *to* your opponent so he or she can also warm up.

During the match:

1. If you are serving, call the score before each point and be sure your opponent is ready before you serve.
2. Call faults on yourself promptly and fairly.
3. Make line decisions correctly; do not ask spectators for help with line decisions and avoid suggesting replays repeatedly.
4. Retrieve shuttles on your side of the net and those nearest you. When you return the shuttle, hit it to your opponent when he or she is ready and do not just shove it under the net.
5. Ask your opponent first if you wish to change or modify the shuttle.
6. Avoid abusive language and racket throwing.
7. Play at your best even if your opponent does not have your expertise. It is insulting to your opponent to do otherwise.

Following the match:

1. Shake hands and thank your opponent.

Tournament Conduct

1. Fill out the tournament entry blank accurately and completely, and return it on time.
2. Plan to arrive at the tournament well before the time of your first match. Report to the tournament desk upon arrival at the tournament, verify the time of your match, and check your opponent's name and the court number.
3. Avoid being late on court for your match. Do not risk being defaulted.
4. Do your stretching and warm up before going on the court, so that you need at most no more than 5 minutes of rallying before beginning.
5. After the match, thank the umpire and find out the time of your next match. If there is no umpire, report the score to the tournament desk.
6. After the tournament, write a thank-you note to the tournament chairman and to any other hosts you may have had.

A Final Word

In all competitive play, learning to win and lose gracefully is essential. Don't blame your defeat or poor play on some trivial matter or excuse. Keep your thoughts to yourself, analyze your play and determine to increase your abilities.

Officiating

The officials needed to conduct a match are an umpire, a service judge, and ten linesmen. National, international, and world championship matches require this full complement of officials. Locally, twelve officials are rarely available until the final round. State and school matches are often played without any officials whatsoever, in which case the players themselves keep score and conduct the match.

Duties of the Officials

The umpire conducts the match, calls the score, rules on receiving faults, and enforces the laws of badminton. The service judge rules on service faults (this chapter, items 12–16). The linesmen determine if the shuttle is inside or outside the line. If the service judge or linesmen cannot make a decision, the umpire may do so.

For those particularly interested in this facet of the game, information can be found in the *USBA Rule Book* or the *IBF Handbook*—see References.

Figure 2.4 shows the position of officials for a match. U refers to the umpire, SJ to the service judge, and L to linesmen.

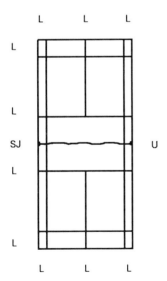

Figure 2.4
Location of officials on court.

Conduct of the Match

1. Only an official has the privilege of communicating with players. The one exception is during the intermission that comes at the end of the second game if a third game is required to determine the winner of the match.
2. Applause at anytime is welcomed but spectators should refrain from making sudden noises while the shuttle is in play.
3. Decisions of the linesmen are final and, in their absence, the umpire in charge will ask if he wishes help at any time on line decisions.

Following is a sample scoresheet used by the umpire (fig. 2.5).

Can you list the officials required for a national championship match? How should players keep track of the score if there are no officials provided for a match?

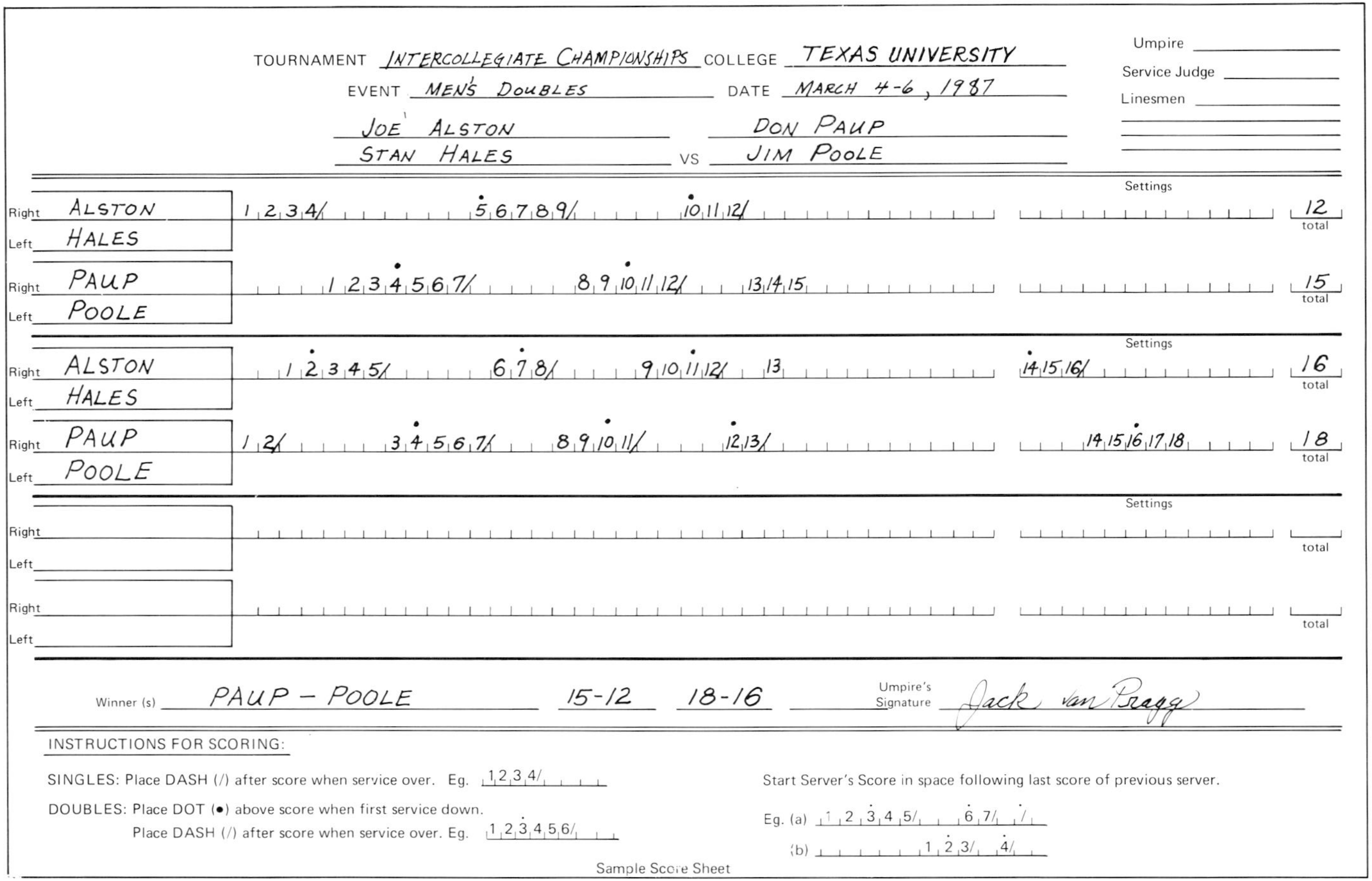

TOURNAMENT _INTERCOLLEGIATE CHAMPIONSHIPS_ COLLEGE _TEXAS UNIVERSITY_

EVENT _MEN'S DOUBLES_ DATE _MARCH 4-6, 1987_

JOE' ALSTON
STAN HALES VS _DON PAUP_
JIM POOLE

Umpire _____
Service Judge _____
Linesmen _____

			Settings	total
Right	ALSTON	1,2,3,4/	.5,6,7,8,9/	.10,11,12/		12
Left	HALES					
Right	PAUP	1,2,3,4,5,6,7/	8,9,10,11,12/	13,14,15		15
Left	POOLE					

			Settings	total
Right	ALSTON	1,2,3,4,5/	6,7,8/	9,10,11,12/	13	14,15,16/	16
Left	HALES					
Right	PAUP	1,2/	3,4,5,6,7/	8,9,10,11/	12,13/	14,15,16,17,18	18
Left	POOLE					

		Settings	total
Right			
Left			
Right			
Left			

total

Winner (s) _PAUP - POOLE_   _15-12   18-16_

Umpire's Signature _Jack van Praag_

INSTRUCTIONS FOR SCORING:

SINGLES: Place DASH (/) after score when service over. Eg. 1,2,3,4/

DOUBLES: Place DOT (•) above score when first service down.
Place DASH (/) after score when service over. Eg. 1,2,3,4,5,6/

Start Server's Score in space following last score of previous server.

Eg. (a) 1,2,3,4,5/ 6,7/ ;
    (b) 1,2,3/ 4/

Sample Score Sheet

Figure 2.5
Sample scoresheet.

Skills for Every Player— Preliminaries

3

Before a beginning badminton player learns the basic shots that are useful in a game of singles or doubles, as well as the stroking techniques employed to produce these shots, it is also necessary to acquire some associated skills that accompany good stroke technique. This chapter describes the skills prerequisite to effective shot production, and chapter 4 describes the basic strokes and shots themselves. Chapter 7 contains instruction on more advanced strokes and shots that should be learned only when one has become familiar with the techniques of this chapter and chapter 4.

Before attempting stroking techniques, you must learn

how to warm up
how to grip your racket
where to position yourself on the court
how to stand when awaiting returns
how to move about the court

How to Warm Up

It takes time to stretch and warm up properly for badminton. Get off to a good start by warming up sufficiently before going on court. Especially when playing competitively, you should increase your body temperature for maximum performance. Before going on court, do the following:

1. Stretch out the muscles and tendons of your legs, stomach, back, and arms by a series of slow exercises while sitting and standing: toe touches, trunk twists, arm circles, etc.
2. Swing the racket while it is still in its cover, simulating the various badminton strokes, especially clears and drives. Start slowly, gradually speeding up the swing.
3. Bounce on your feet and run in place to get your legs limber.
4. Practice quick starts with footwork similar to that on court.
5. Take quick, short sprints—forward, backward, side to side, and diagonally.

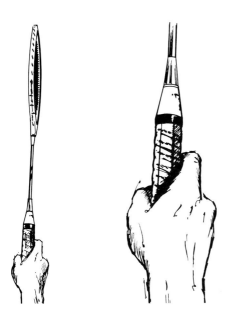

Figure 3.1
Forehand grip.

How to Grip Your Racket

Most badminton strokes are executed with either a forehand or backhand grip. Strokes made overhead or on the right side of the body require a forehand grip. Strokes made on the left side of the body require a backhand grip. (These suggestions and instructions and others of a similar nature throughout the book pertain to right-handed players. Left-handed players should in each case use the side opposite to that cited.)

Forehand Grip

Examine your badminton racket handle. Notice that it has eight sides or bevels. The top bevel is the side of the handle which is visible when the racket head is held at right angles to the ground, as shown in figure 3.1. Here are five points to remember in holding the racket for this grip:

1. The point of the V formed by your thumb and forefinger is at the left edge of the top bevel of the handle (fig. 3.1).
2. Hold the racket in your fingers, and not just in your palm like a hammer. Lay the racket across your fingers and palm, and let your little finger maintain a firm hold (fig. 3.2).
3. Spread your fingers so they are comfortable, particularly the forefinger and middle finger. Use your thumb and forefinger to control the racket.

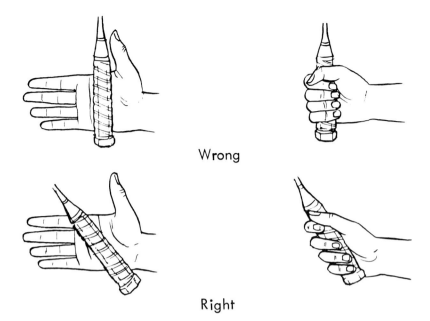

Wrong

Right

Figure 3.2
Use of the fingers on the grip.

4. Hold the racket near the end of the handle. This allows more wrist action. Do not let the butt of the handle extend beyond the heel of your hand, except in special circumstances when "choking up" is necessary for quick response.
5. When you execute "power" shots, hold the racket firmly at impact. On "touch" shots, hold the racket more loosely.

To get a comfortable feeling it may be necessary to adjust this basic grip by spreading or closing your fingers, by moving your hand closer to the end, or by resting the end of the handle at a comfortable place on the heel of your hand.

Remember: The position of the V should not be changed.

Backhand Grip

For this grip (for shots played on the left side of the body), remember these three points (fig. 3.3):

1. Turn your hand counterclockwise until the point of the V is on the top left bevel.
2. On drives and clears, place the ball (or first joint) of your thumb flat against the back bevel of the handle. This position gives the support necessary for power and depth.
3. Dropshots and net shots require control rather than power, so it is not necessary to have your thumb flat. It may rest across the back bevel as it does on the forehand.

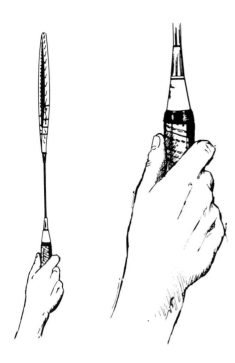

Figure 3.3
Backhand grip.

How is the backhand grip for a net shot changed to perform a backhand high clear? Why is this change in hand position advocated?

Where to Position Yourself on the Court

The center location is your basic position in singles play. This is the location on the court from which you are able to reach most shots easily. Here, you command the best area for any maneuver.

The center location is halfway between the net and back boundary line and on the center line, halfway between the sidelines (fig. 3.4).

Your opponent will try to draw you from this basic center position by directing the shuttle to a corner. Your strategy is to retrieve the corner shots but return quickly to the center position.

How to Stand When Awaiting Returns

To ready yourself for each of your opponent's strokes, practice these five points consciously, until they become habit (fig. 3.5):

1. Take a position in the center of the court. Stand alertly with your weight evenly distributed on the balls of your feet.
2. Stand with your feet side-by-side and apart just enough to give good balance, but not so far apart that movement is restricted.

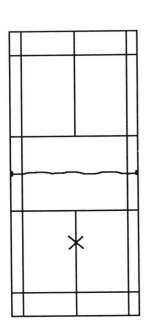

Figure 3.4
Center or base position for singles.

Figure 3.5
Ready position.

3. Relax your body, and flex your knees slightly; do not be stiff and upright. Be ready for instantaneous action.
4. Carry both your arms in front of your body, with the racket acting almost as a shield. Hold the racket head up about shoulder height and away from you, in order to allow a swift stroke.
5. Concentrate on the shuttle as it leaves your opponent's racket, and try to determine the direction of the shot. As soon as you determine the direction, move your feet and pivot your body by the time the shuttle crosses the net.

All players vary the ready position somewhat to suit their own style and comfort. Champions adjust it to give them the greatest mobility and quickness. Quickness refers not only to feet and hands but to eyes and brains as well. The shuttle has such a short distance to travel that it will come swiftly and offer you little time to execute the fundamentals.

In fact, in badminton, absolutely no time is available to pause and survey the situation. Even in doubles, where your partner covers half the court, you must be ready for every shot. Points are made because opponents have neither the time nor the reflexes to get their rackets in position to return the shuttle.

Why do you suppose it is important not to be moving when your opponent hits the shuttlecock?

How to Move About the Court

In order to get within reach of the shuttlecock and to conserve energy in the process, good footwork is essential. Powerful and deceptive strokes are of little use if a player is not in the correct place soon enough to stroke the shuttle effectively.

Essentials of Good Footwork

1. The beginning of good footwork is an alert starting position. Keep the body ready to move in any direction by flexing the knees slightly with your weight on the forward part of your feet. Think "ready." A stiff upright stance does not permit speed.
2. Badminton footwork is best described as "springing sideways and gliding to the shuttle." Keep your feet close to the floor.
3. It is very important not to be moving when your opponent hits the shuttle. If you cannot get completely back to the center of the court, pause where you are before your opponent hits the shuttle.

Moving to the Baseline

4. To prepare for a forehand overhead stroke in the deep right court, lead with your right foot and take gliding steps diagonally back to the corner. Finish with your left side partially turned toward the net. Your left foot is forward as you hit (fig. 3.6).
5. To prepare for a backhand stroke from the deep left court, turn on the left foot and stride diagonally back to the corner with your back partially turned to the net. Your right foot is out in front of you, pointed sideways or diagonally to the corner (fig. 3.7).

Moving to the Net

6. To move to either corner at net, push off with your left foot and lead with your right. The second step is with your left foot, and the third step lands you with the right foot in front (figs. 3.8 and 3.9).

Practice moving from center court to the right and left sidelines and to the baseline until you are consistent in the number of steps taken for a given direction. How many steps do you require to play the shuttle from each of the boundary lines?

Right foot is the racket foot in badminton. Unlike tennis, most shots are played "off" the right foot (that is, the right leg and foot have the weight on them at the moment of contact) even when playing shots on the right side of the court. This allows for better reach, without getting too far from the center of the court. After playing the shot, let your left leg share the load by using it to push off back toward center position.

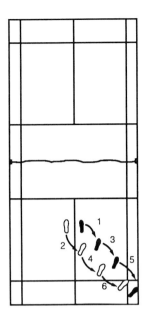

Figure 3.6
Footwork to deep forehand corner.

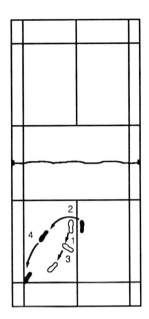

Figure 3.7
Footwork to deep backhand corner.

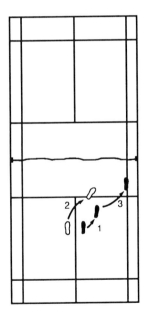

Figure 3.8
Footwork to front forehand corner.

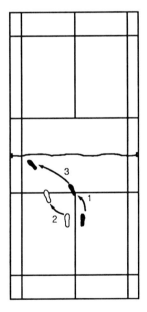

Figure 3.9
Footwork to front backhand corner.

As your footwork skills become more proficient, the number of steps from center to all parts of the court can be determined. The footwork then becomes a pattern. Learning to judge whether or not a shuttle is going out of bounds on the baseline and sidelines is made easier when the footwork becomes measured. The easiest part of badminton footwork is, of course, running forward. Because the basic waiting position is in the center of the court, however, backward and sideward steps are also required. Moving backward is called "backpedaling." It is a skill demanded in other sports, too. The football quarterback backpedals almost every time he takes the ball from the center.

So it is with the badminton player. Keep your head and eyes forward at all times. If you have to turn and run with your back to the net, you will not have enough time to turn again to stroke the shuttle.

Good footwork combined with early anticipation of the direction and depth of the shuttlecock should place the player *behind* the shuttle. This enables a move forward and a hit into the shot. Sluggish footwork often results in the shuttle getting behind the player, resulting in a poorly executed stroke. (The only exception to this is the deep backhand, which is best hit from slightly behind the body.) Good footwork is not only important in returning high deep clears but essential for an effective return of a high deep serve.

In playing a shot from the right corner at net, which foot should be forward as you stroke the shuttlecock and why?

Skills for Every Player—
Elementary Strokes and Shots

4

Mastering the fundamental stroking techniques and basic shots of badminton involves the following:

underhand strokes—the serve
                     —the underhand clear and dropshot
overhead strokes—the clear
                —the dropshot
                —the smash
sidearm stroke—the drive
net play—the hairpin drop

Underhand Strokes

The Serve

Underhand strokes are all those in which the contact point and the head of the racket are below the level of the hand. The contact point is below net level which necessitates an upward stroke (fig. 4.1).

Begin play with the serve, an underhand stroke. Play it underhand forehand or underhand backhand, although underhand forehand is the usual method. The shaft of the racket must point downward so that the whole of the head of the racket is discernibly below the hand holding the racket (figs. 2.3 and 4.2).

Basic Singles Serve

1. Take a comfortable position in the court about three feet behind the short service line and to the right or left of the center line.
2. Stand with your feet spread but not so far apart that you cannot move quickly. Your left foot should be in advance of your right foot.
3. Both feet must remain in contact with the floor until you contact the shuttle. Once you put your racket in motion to serve, neither foot may slide during the entire execution of the stroke.
4. Hold the shuttle at the base between your thumb and forefinger of your left hand (or use both fore and middle fingers). Extend your left arm forward about level with your shoulders (fig. 4.2).
5. Hold the racket with a forehand grip with your wrist cocked. Bring the racket behind your body at about waist level. This is the starting position. Then drop or toss the shuttle in front of you.

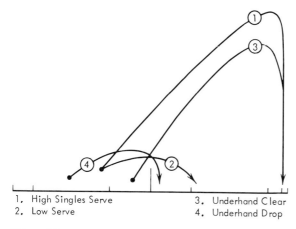

1. High Singles Serve   3. Underhand Clear
2. Low Serve   4. Underhand Drop

Figure 4.1
Flight patterns produced by underhand strokes.

Figure 4.2
Serve.

6. Swing the racket forward, uncock the wrist, and let the racket and shuttle meet ahead of your body between knee and waist level.
7. Rapidly rotate the forearm and wrist inward immediately prior to contact. Most strokes in badminton are made with a similar rotating movement.
8. The follow-through goes in the direction that you intend the shuttle to go, that is, high and deep. Avoid bringing the racket up to the shuttle. Let the shuttle drop. Otherwise an outright miss or a wood shot (hitting the frame of the racket) will result (fig. 4.3).

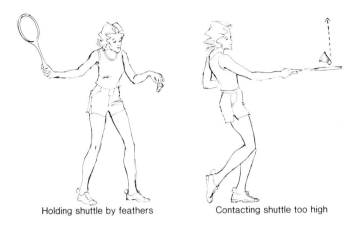

Holding shuttle by feathers   Contacting shuttle too high

Figure 4.3
Mistakes most commonly made with the serve.

The Low Serve

The low serve is used primarily in doubles and with great variation. It is also used as a change of pace in singles. The grips and stance are usually the same as for the singles serve, but the racket pattern and use of the wrist vary widely. Of all the strokes in badminton, the low serve technique has the most variables. The swing is often shortened and the stroke made almost entirely with your forearm guiding the shuttle. Most players prefer an exceptionally firm wrist believing it gives more control. This is one stroke a player must experiment with and find the style best suited for him. Try for accuracy in having the shuttle go over the top of the net with minimum clearance. If your low serve forces the receiver to hit up it is a highly successful serve. If the receiver "rushes" your low serve and is able to hit it on the downswing, change your technique and practice it more.

Placement Areas

The serve can be directed high or low, short or long. Figure 4.4 shows the specific areas within the service court to which the shuttle can be served most effectively.

In singles there should be no noticeable difference in the way one produces low and high serves, as here again deception is important in order to keep your opponent in doubt as to which it will be (and off balance). Basically, the high serve is used more often in singles and the low serve more often in doubles. Occasionally mixing them keeps your opponent uncertain and unable to predict your pattern. It is imperative that you serve well, as serving gives you the opportunity to score.

Even though somewhat alike in production, the low and high serves are different. They can be compared with the dropshot and clear in wrist action and needed power. The low serve takes little power and is almost guided over the net whereas the high, deep serve will take all the strength and power available to get

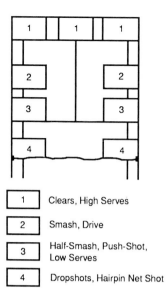

1	Clears, High Serves
2	Smash, Drive
3	Half-Smash, Push-Shot, Low Serves
4	Dropshots, Hairpin Net Shot

Figure 4.4
Placement areas.

the shuttle high enough and deep enough to be considered successful. The latter has much the same flight as the clear because it is hit to a point high above the backcourt and when it loses speed it turns and falls straight down. If the shuttle falls straight down on the back boundary line, the opponent must be that far back in the court to return it. If it is too flat and too low, the receiver will intercept it before it ever gets to the backcourt.

Conversely, the shuttle hit with a low serve has a flat arc as it just skims over the net and into the court near the short service line.

The low serve in doubles requires the same grip and foot position. However, the backswing is shortened, the shuttle contacted as near waist level as possible and perhaps slightly more to the right. The shuttle is guided over the net without wrist motion. A great deal less shoulder, arm, and wrist power will be needed to hit the short distance and low trajectory required for the low serve.

Because the serve is played underhand and therefore must be hit upward, it is considered a defensive stroke. Consequently, in order to score, the server must eventually turn his defense into an attack. Since the receiver cannot score a point, his objective is to stay on the attack and win the opportunity to serve, making it possible then for him to score. This peculiarity of badminton—having to score from a beginning defensive position—prolongs a game even though no points are recorded.

In most sports the serve is considered an attacking stroke. Why is this not the case in badminton?

Underhand Clear

Many of the same stroke production fundamentals of the high, deep, singles serve—the grip, the wrist and arm power, and the follow-through—can be applied to the underhand clear. When stroking this clear, swing the racket down from the ready position, under the shuttle for contact and up, following through in the intended direction of the shuttle. Except for the fact that it originates near the net, the flight pattern the shuttle makes mimics the high, deep serve. Note figure 4.1.

Just as with the overhead defensive clear (see below), use the underhand clear to gain time to recover the center position and to force the opponent to the backcourt. The underhand clear's values are many in both singles and doubles. For example, if a dropshot is not particularly good and does not fall close to the net, a large choice of shots is available. Near-perfect dropshots necessitate a return with an underhand clear, in which case this stroke becomes indispensable. The only alternative to using the underhand clear is the hairpin net shot described on page 50.

Underhand Dropshot

The underhand dropshot described here is played from an area between the short service line and the baseline to the opponent's side of the net as near to the net as possible. It has specific use both in singles and doubles.

Closely related, and yet different in its usage, is the dropshot played closer to the net (fig. 4.1). The fundamentals of stroking and the characteristics of the underhand dropshot are almost identical with those of the low serve. A slow, controlled shot, the dropshot has its limitations for this reason: if you hit the shuttle from the baseline at a slow pace, your opponent has time to pounce on it at the net. Unless the underhand dropshot is disguised, ineffective returns result. Although rarely played successfully from the baseline, this stroke's values are exceptional in doubles and mixed doubles when played from midcourt. In doubles, the dropshot is used to run the net player from side to side or to draw a player up when both players are back. In singles, it can be a superb return of a smash. Directed crosscourt away from the smasher, the dropshot forces him to recover quickly and to run the long distance.

Overhead Strokes

The Clear

The overhead stroke is very similar to the motion of throwing a baseball. The most basic badminton shot hit with this stroke is the clear—a high shot deep to the back of the opponent's court. The high clear is a defensive shot, used to recover or gain time. A variation, the attacking clear, is an effective offensive shot (fig. 4.5).

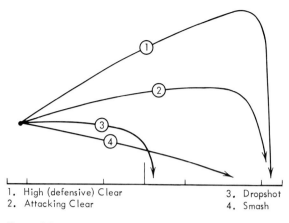

1. High (defensive) Clear   3. Dropshot
2. Attacking Clear   4. Smash

Figure 4.5
Flight patterns produced by overhead strokes.

Procedure

1. Take the proper forehand grip, watch the approaching shuttle, and use the prescribed footwork. Move yourself to a place where you are in correct relationship to the shuttle.
2. As you are moving to this position behind the shuttle, swing your racket and arm back behind your head and shoulders. This will require pivoting at your waist and turning your shoulders sideways to the net. This position is fundamentally the same as that taken by a baseball outfielder making an overarm throw to home plate. In badminton the racket, instead of the ball, is in your hand, but it is literally thrown at the shuttle in the identical fashion.
3. Rotate your forearm and wrist inward as you move the racket from behind your head. This rotation, called pronation, continues through the entire stroke.
4. Incorrectly allowing your arm to drop and bend when stroking results in loss of power. With full power, contact the shuttle with your arm fully extended and ahead of your body.
5. Rotate your trunk forward during this stroke to gain power.
6. Your ideal position is behind and in line with the shuttle.
7. Always hit the shuttle as soon as possible so that your opponent will not have time to get your shots.
8. Meet the shuttle with a flat racket or surface without any cutting or slicing motion. Cutting gives control but takes away power.

Here are some additional suggestions for achieving a successful clear.

1. Since the shuttlecock is difficult to slice because of its feathers and does not react as a spinning ball, it is essential to learn how to exert power.
2. The contact of the racket and shuttle must be quite explosive to get distance since there is little weight on the racket.

Figure 4.6
Overhead clear.

3. The angle of the racket face upon contact is the final determining factor as to the direction the shuttle will take.
4. Be sure to move your weight into the shot as the stroke is made.
5. Note the flight pattern of the clear in figure 4.5. The shuttle is hit high enough so that at a certain point, almost above the back boundary line, it loses speed and turns and falls straight down. A shuttle falling at right angles to the floor is most difficult to play. It is important to hit the shuttle with depth because your opponent will be unable to smash a clear effectively from the back boundary line.

High Clear Strategy

The high or defensive clear is used primarily to gain time for the player to return to the center position in the court. One of the most valuable benefits of this shot is derived from its use in combinations with the dropshot to run your opponent, making him defend all four corners of the court.

As can be seen in figure 4.5, depth and height of the shuttlecock are extremely important on the defensive clear in order to force your opponent as far into the backcourt as possible.

Your next shot, a dropshot just over the net, would become very effective in this game of maneuvering for openings and spaces. It might also force your opponent to hit a short return which could be smashed. It takes a strong player to clear from one baseline to the opposite one and an extraordinarily strong player to high clear crosscourt to the diagonal corner. Unless a shuttle that flies very fast is used, it is unlikely that the average player would be able to accomplish this difficult feat. Consequently, in singles, the player who hits a high deep defensive clear gains control of the rally and should eventually win that point.

Analyzing a match played by contestants of equal skill demonstrates that the player who consistently has good length always wins. When playing, if you find you do not have time to reach the shots and each point is a struggle then check the length of your clears. Your opponent will seldom return a winning shot or putaway if your clear is deep enough. Also, clears that are too low and too short are cut off before they reach the backcourt.

The Attacking Clear

After learning the basic high deep clear, the attacking clear, a modification, can be developed. Its use should not be confused with that of the defensive clear or disaster will result.

1. The trajectory of the attacking clear is not as high but it is faster. There is a different arc to the flight pattern, as can be seen in figure 4.5.
2. Because the arc is low, the attacking clear can be used more successfully when the opponent is out of center position.
3. Often the attacking clear is best used following a good dropshot to the forehand corner. The clear can then be hit quickly to the backhand corner while the opponent is recovering from the net.

Contacting the shuttle too late

Standing flat to the net

Figure 4.7
Mistakes most commonly made with the overhead clear.

4. Once the clear gets behind the opponent on the backhand, the return is more likely to be in the forecourt. When an opponent's return is forced to be short, the point should be yours! A defensive clear incorrectly used in this situation would give the opponent time to move back and hit overhead, and your advantage would be lost.

The only difference in the production of these two types of clears is that the attacking clear has a flatter arc; therefore, stroke it with less upward angle. It also requires more power, since without the upward angle, it would not travel far enough.

The Overhead Dropshot

The dropshot is a slow shot that drops just over the net in the opponent's forecourt.

Procedure

1. Use exactly the same grip, footwork, body position, and backswing described for the overhead clear. Indeed, your intention should be to suggest that a clear is forthcoming.
2. The difference is wrist speed. There is less wrist rotation, and the shuttle is stroked with greater control rather than "patted."
3. Contact the shuttle farther ahead of your body in order to direct it downward.
4. The downward movement of your arm coupled with completion of your wrist action brings the shuttle down. Tilt the face of the racket downward at the angle you wish the shuttle to take.
5. Rotate your shoulder and trunk forward and move your weight into the shot (fig. 4.8).

Advantages of a Dropshot

1. A dropshot is invaluable because it enables you to use the front corners of the court. No other type of shot goes to the two front corners near the net.
2. The smash and drive are placed midcourt or deeper as shown in figures 4.5 and 4.13. Always place the dropshot in the forecourt. The dropshot, whether overhead, underhand or hit from the side, can be played from any place on the court.

Dropshot Strategy

1. A major part of singles strategy lies in using the overhead dropshot in combination with clears. For example, if clears are used repeatedly, a player tends to move his basic position toward the rear of the court in order to cover the deep shots. This position makes the dropshot doubly effective.
2. Singles becomes a game of up and back and up and back again until a weak return is forced and a smash finishes the rally.

Figure 4.8
Overhead dropshot.

3. A midcourt shot, one which is halfway between the net and back boundary line, obviously is not as useful in singles as in doubles, since these shots do not move the opponent out of center. Consequently, keep the shuttle as far from the center of the court as possible with clears and drops.

4. Deception is the most outstanding characteristic of a good dropshot. If the dropshot is deceptive enough it can be an outright winner even though it might have been planned as a lead-up shot.

5. If your opponent is halfway to the net or at the net before your shot reaches the net, then you haven't fooled him and you have probably lost the exchange.

6. As you become more skilled with the dropshot, experiment by hitting it fast or slow and with more or less arc. Try slicing the shuttle slightly in order to slow it down and change its direction. This will very much add to the deception of the shot.

7. The least attractive characteristic of the dropshot is its slow flight. Anything moving slowly unfortunately gives your opponent what you don't want him to have—time. The dropshot, however, contributes to the essence of the game—measuring time and selecting shots in relation to your own and your opponent's position on the court.

Can you name the two most important characteristics of a good dropshot?

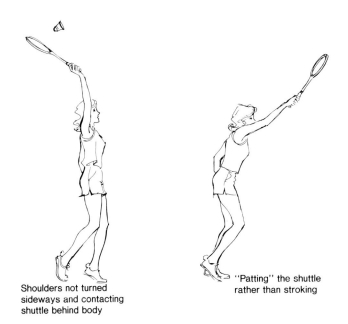

Shoulders not turned
sideways and contacting
shuttle behind body

"Patting" the shuttle
rather than stroking

Figure 4.9
Mistakes most commonly made with the overhead dropshot.

The Smash

The smash is a powerful overhead shot used to "put away" any shuttle above the height of the net.

1. In the interest of deception, the smash should be masked as a clear or a drop. Use the same grip, footwork, body position, backswing, and contact point as with the clear and the drop, and your opponent will not anticipate your return.
2. The smash differs from the clear and the dropshot in that it can be hit only with an overhead stroke; a clear and a dropshot can come from either an overhead or underhand stroke.
3. Be sure you move yourself to a position behind the shuttle as quickly as possible.
4. Take care to have a proper body position, since balance must be perfect to achieve maximum power from your shoulders, arms, and wrist. Your left shoulder must be turned to the net and your right shoulder back and ready to strike with force.
5. Cock your arm and wrist behind your body ready to unleash all available power. The racket head may be moving at a terrific rate as it goes out to meet the shuttle. The handle must be gripped quite firmly at the instant of contact.
6. Contact the shuttle at the highest comfortable point. The follow-through is down and in line with the flight of the shuttle.

7. Hit the overhead smash with as much power as that needed for the high, deep clear. To get such power, rotate the wrist and forearm fully and rapidly and use perfect timing.
8. Rotate your trunk and shoulders forward and throw your weight into the shot. When you are first learning to smash, however, try to get your timing and downward angle correct before attempting to get excessive speed. Timing is thrown off if too much arm and body effort are involved in the stroke; let a swiftly rotating racket do the work.
9. The racket face must be angled downward at contact point to make the shuttle travel sharply downward.
10. It is important to remember that the farther away you are from the net, the less angle and speed the smash can carry.

Strategy

Two reasons for using a smash are:

1. It has more downward angle and speed than any other stroke, making it the main point-winning shot. If the pattern of play has developed as planned, your final shot of the rally will be an overhead smash.
2. If the smash is returned, the return will be (because of the angle of your smash) an upward (defensive) stroke.

Obviously, in both situations, the smash is an invaluable weapon. There is, however, a reason for avoiding indiscriminate use of the smash, namely, the effort needed to smash leaves your body off balance, and therefore it takes longer to recover your position than with other types of shots. Thus, your judgment as to when to smash rather than to clear or to drop is important. Many factors related to you and to your opponent will enter into this decision.

It is interesting to note the characteristics which are alike in making the various shots. Examine figures 4.6, 4.8, and 4.10. The position of the feet and the body is the same for all overhead shots. The stroke pattern—backswing, forward swing, and follow-through—should also be almost identical for the overhead strokes in order to employ the deception necessary to make the shots effective. What, then, determines whether an overhead shot is to be a clear, a dropshot, or a smash?

The answer lies in the speed of the wrist, the degree of wrist action used, and the angle of the face of the racket at the moment of contact with the shuttle. On all badminton shots, cock the wrist back ready for the action that comes within the larger action of the shoulder and arm swing. Wrist power alone is not sufficient to propel the shuttle from one end of the court to the other; it necessitates arm power and shoulder rotation in addition to exact timing of the wrist snap as the weight moves forward. When a player intends to smash and put the shuttle "away," he may leap off the ground for better angle and possible added power. In this case, he is not using any deception to enhance the stroke. Total energy is being called upon instead.

Which stroke and which flight path require the greatest power in badminton?

Figure 4.10
Smash.

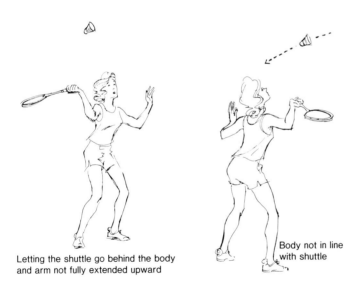

Letting the shuttle go behind the body
and arm not fully extended upward

Body not in line
with shuttle

Figure 4.11
Mistakes most commonly made with the smash.

The Half-Paced Smash

The half-paced smash, popularly called "half-smash," is simply a smash with less speed. All elements of stroke production related to the smash apply to the half-smash. It is important to keep the following points in mind:

1. The half-smash is played by contacting the shuttle with an extended arm diagonally above the head in order to obtain a steep angle downward.
2. To cut or slice the half-smash diminishes its speed and makes the shuttle fall close to the net at a sharper angle.
3. If the shuttle gets behind the player, the racket will be facing upward at contact point, the flight of the shuttle will be upward, and the shot will be a defensive one, in all probability a clear. It is important, therefore, that the shuttle be contacted well ahead of the body.
4. Caution: A smash hit with a bent arm results in loss of power and angle. The smash is then known as a "flat" smash, a highly undesirable shot.

The half-smash has as many values as the full, powerful smash, but is of a different nature. The half-smash can be played with less effort. Moreover, it can be played from deeper in the court since recovery of balance does not present a problem. Moving to cover the net return after the half-smash can be accomplished with ease. By contrast, a full smash from the backcourt leaves the front corners vulnerable. The use of the half-smash therefore is less risky. It is valuable, too, because of its sharply angled downward direction. By hitting downward, the attack is gained by forcing the opponent to stroke upward. Very few points are won outright from an underhand stroke. The ones that are can be attributed to outright deception or to outpositioning the opponent.

It is desirable to deceive your opponent as to whether you intend to make a dropshot, clear, or smash. How can this be done?

Angle of the Racket Face

The direction of the shuttle's flight in all overhead shots is determined by the angle of the racket face. Bringing the wrist and racket head through too soon causes as extreme downward angle to the shuttle, often resulting in a netted shot. Conversely, failure to bring the wrist and racket head through soon enough causes an extreme upward angle (fig. 4.12).

Sidearm Strokes

The Drive

The drive is produced by a flat sidearm stroke played on the forehand or backhand. See figure 4.13 for flights of sidearm strokes.

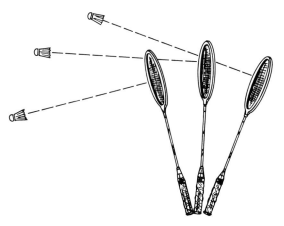

Figure 4.12
Angle of racket face.

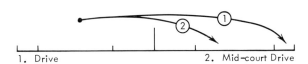

1. Drive   2. Mid-court Drive

Figure 4.13
Flight patterns produced by sidearm strokes.

Forehand Drive

The forehand drive is played on the right side of the body and is similar to the baseball sidearm throw (fig. 4.14).

1. Take a forehand grip, turn your body until your left shoulder is to the net, and turn your shoulders to allow your arm to take the backswing.
2. Place the head of the racket between your shoulder blades. To start the backswing, bend your elbow and cock your wrist backward in preparation for a big, powerful swing.
3. Watch the shuttle closely with the idea of contacting it diagonally ahead between shoulder and waist height.
4. As your arm and racket swing forward, your body weight should transfer from your right foot to your left foot. Rotate your forearm and wrist inward during the stroke.
5. Contact the shuttle with a flat racket face and well away from you so that your swing is not restricted.
6. Swing the racket on through in the direction of the flight of the shuttle. The speed of your swing compels the racket to complete its follow-through past the left shoulder. The racket has practically made a 360° circle. The action of the swing, particularly in the contact area, is explosive.
7. On many occasions, the forehand drive is played with the *right* foot extended toward the sideline. This allows for a further reach without getting too far from the center position.

Figure 4.14
Forehand drive.

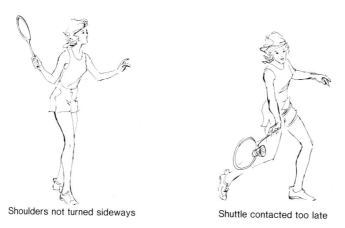

Shoulders not turned sideways   Shuttle contacted too late

Figure 4.15
Mistakes most commonly made with the forehand drive.

Backhand Drive

The backhand drive employs the same basic principles as the forehand drive with two or three exceptions:

1. The grip is changed to the backhand grip, making sure that your thumb is flat on the handle. Now, rotate your forearm and wrist outward.
2. Elbow rotation is important in this and all other strokes. On the backswing your elbow is bent, your right hand is at your left shoulder, and your elbow is pointing at the oncoming shuttle.
3. Your weight shifts, your shoulders turn, your arm starts swinging forward with your elbow leading, and then the head of the racket whips over for the contact and follow-through.

Figure 4.16
Backhand drive.

Elbow not pointing at shuttle   Contacting the shuttle too late

Figure 4.17
Mistakes most commonly made with the backhand drive.

Playing the Drives

Long, deep, fast drives and slower-paced midcourt drives can be played from either side of the body. Drives can be played like other shots, from one sideline diagonally across the court to the other sideline (crosscourt) or they can be played parallel to the sideline (down-the-line). The flight pattern of the drive is parallel to the floor and the shuttle just skims the net (fig. 4.13). The drive is played anywhere from midcourt to backcourt and is driven to your opponent's deep court or midcourt depending on his location in the court at the moment.

The higher you can contact the shuttle on the drive, the less you will have to hit up. For example, if you hit the shuttle from below knee level it will have to go up to get over the net and will continue to rise as it carries on to midcourt.

If the shuttle rises to net level and then turns toward the floor because speed is lost, you have mistakenly hit a dropshot. Any shot higher than net level can be smashed and therein lies the danger of the hard-hit drive played from a low contact point. A drive less powerful (midcourt) may be of value if your opponent is not pulled out of position. The shuttle's arc will reach its peak at the net and descend from there on to midcourt. It therefore cannot be smashed.

Try never to provide your opponent with a set-up for a smash.

Use the fast drive when an opponent is out of position and you wish to get the shuttle behind him to the backcourt. Perhaps you hit a well-placed dropshot to his forehand. The deep backhand corner is now briefly open. If your opponent returns your dropshot to your forehand, your problem is simple. If he plays it down-the-line to your backhand, it is not so simple. You must get the shuttle there quickly before he gains the center of the court or he will block the shot off for a winner while you are still recovering from the execution of your stroke. It takes more time to recover body balance and center position from hard-hit power shots than from dropshots, midcourt drives, or net shots.

If the two kinds of drive are used correctly and intelligently, they can be valuable attacking weapons. Used badly, they can cause disaster.

Angle of the Racket Face

The direction of the shuttle's flight is determined by the angle of the racket face. It will require a great deal of practice to learn to control the moment of impact of the racket head and the shuttle in order to direct shots down-the-line or cross-court.

Net Play

Description

Net play is a general term encompassing those shots played from the area around the short service line to the net (fig. 4.18). Net play, which includes the hairpin net shot described in this chapter as well as the push shot and the net smash described in chapter 7, is very important because the front of the court has to be defended.

The forehand grip is generally satisfactory for net play but the backhand grip must be adjusted slightly:

1. The side of the thumb is placed up the back bevel of the racket which may cause a slight turning of the hand toward the forehand grip.
2. The wrist is used differently for net shots, that is, with little relationship to the shoulders and body. The grip adjustment allows such wrist action. Conversely, this grip could not be used successfully to perform a clear from the backhand corner.

Figure 4.18
Net play.

On both forehand and backhand strokes, spread the fingers and hold the racket almost loosely. This should give more "touch." To get even more control, hold the racket slightly up from the end. This shortening of the grip gives less power (not needed at net) and less reach. You must decide, therefore, what you wish to gain (control) and what you wish to sacrifice (reach).

The feet, body, and upper arm are used for reaching rather than for stroke production; the actual strokes are done with the forearm, wrist, and hand. The racket meets the shuttle with a flat face. The wrist action may be smooth and controlled or it may be quick, depending on the type of net shot you are attempting. The explosive power so essential for clears and smashes is not needed in the forecourt.

The follow-through should be in the direction in which you wish the shuttle to travel. Guide it and go with it. At times, the follow-through must be abbreviated to avoid hitting the net. According to the rules, a player may not hit the net as long as the shuttle is in play. It is in play until it hits the net or floor.

Your court position for net play in singles and doubles should be such that your extended arm and racket can just touch the net. This distance from the net will permit unrestricted movement of your arm. In doubles it will also enable you to cover more midcourt shots.

In net play take fast, small steps which allow you to turn and move quickly in any direction. The right foot should be forward on all net shots.

The most difficult shots to play at net are those which are falling perpendicular to the floor rather than diagonally. Diagonally dropping shuttles arrive farther back in the court; perpendicular falling shuttles, at their best, touch or almost touch the net as they fall toward the floor. These are extremely difficult to play, and since they cannot be directed forward, only upward, they are called hairpin net shots. Your opponent, sensing this, is alert to smash as soon as the shuttle comes up and over the net.

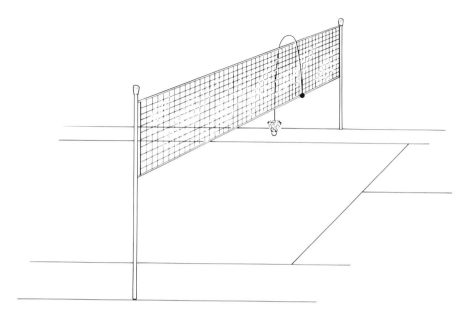

Figure 4.19
Hairpin drop.

Hairpin Net Shot

The hairpin net shot gets its name from the flight pattern of the shuttle (fig. 4.19). Played from one side of the net to the other, it should fall perpendicular to the floor and close to the net on the opponent's side. This shot travels the least distance of any badminton shot; consequently, very little stroke is needed. The shuttle played at net level may be tapped or blocked back. Played well below net level, it will have to be stroked with great care up and over the net. Some championship players stroke the shuttle with a slicing action which gives the shuttle less speed and a spinning motion that is difficult to return. The perfect hairpin shot results in the shuttle's crawling up and over the net and trickling down the other side.

A Final Word on Strokes and Shots

With all strokes, the learning process is the slow, gradual one of getting increased accuracy, further depth, and additional speed. As you continue to play and practice, the shuttle will travel increasingly more often in the direction in which you aim it. You will attain more and more power in clears and smashes and (desirably) less and less speed in dropshots. To further help you stroke your shots effectively and with care, correctly executed basic positions and footwork must precede the actual stroke production. The entire process, then, is one of smooth coordination. Chapter 6 contains a series of drills that offer repetitive practice for all the shots in this chapter.

In every sport involving eye-hand contact, there is one fundamental principle which cannot be overemphasized. In the case of golf or tennis it is "keep your eye on the ball." In badminton it is "keep your eye on the shuttlecock." If you do not watch the shuttlecock, one of the following mistakes will occur:

1. You will miss the shuttlecock entirely.
2. You will hit the feathers of the shuttlecock.
3. You will not hit the shuttle in the center of the racket, thus causing a throw, sling, or a carry.

What is the role of the feet, body, and upper arm when executing a net shot?

Strategies and Tactics

5

Certain strategies and tactics apply to all forms of badminton—singles, doubles, or mixed doubles. Strategies are "plans made for accomplishing an end"; tactics are "skillful devices" for carrying out these plans. In this chapter, both strategies and tactics of badminton are discussed in the following areas:

offense and defense
angle of return
crosscourt shots
receiving serve
singles play
doubles play
mixed doubles play

Winning badminton is generally a question of playing basic fundamentals better than your opponent and understanding and applying strategic principles.

Offense and Defense

In offensive play, shots are directed downward. They are point winning shots such as smashes, half-smashes, dropshots, and low serves. Winning a point from an overhead position requires speed, sharp angles, and accurate direction. However, winning a point from an underhand stroke has to be accomplished through deception or superior court positioning.

In defensive play, shots are directed upward. These shots include the clear, underhand dropshots, and high serves. Drives, being shots with a horizontal trajectory, can be offensive or defensive, depending on their angle of return and on the position of the opponent(s). Offensive and defensive positions may change during the course of a rally. Defense can be changed to offense and vice versa, depending on how well a stroke is executed and selected for use at the proper time. For example, if you return a smash with an underhand hairpin net shot properly angled away from the smasher and the shot falls close to the net, the smasher is forced to hit up (defensive). If, however, the smash had been returned with an underhand clear or weak net shot, the offensive would have remained with the smasher.

Offensive players take chances and strive for outright winners, whereas defensive players are content to "play it safe" and wait for the opponent to err.

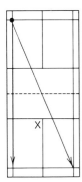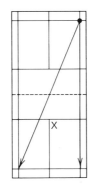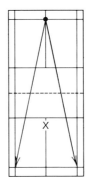

Figure 5.1
Angles of return and base position.

Angle of Return

The angle of return is as important in badminton as it is in tennis and other racket games. It is the angle the returned shuttle takes in relation to the court boundaries. It does not refer to upward or downward angle.

To avoid being trapped by angle of return, position yourself on the court where the greater percentages of returns are likely to come. Occasionally you can neglect a portion of the court, a situation you strive for. This is a form of intelligent anticipation.

Examples: (See figure 5.1).

1. A high clear to your opponent's deep forehand or backhand corner can rarely be returned crosscourt high and deep to your diagonal corner because of the long distance. It could be returned with a flat, fast clear toward that corner, but you will be in the center blocking it before it reaches the intended spot.
2. A shot played to the center of the opponent's court will place the center of the angle of return on the center line.

The best plan is to maintain your position in the center of the angle of possible returns and then be alert to the odd shot.

Crosscourt Shots

Crosscourting and angle of return are closely related. Crosscourt shots travel a longer distance across the court and take more time to reach the intended spot than down-the-line shots. Down-the-line shots travel a shorter distance and are more logical, but more obvious. For example, if you play the shuttle to your opponent's forehand side, anticipate the straight return to your backhand side. Your opponent can crosscourt to your forehand side, but the longer distance gives you more time to reach it.

Crosscourt when you are on balance and are able to return to center quickly and/or when the opponent has overanticipated.

1. A crosscourt shot of any kind played from forehand to forehand leaves the vulnerable backhand exposed.
2. Most of the time move about a foot to the side of the court to which you have directed the shuttle.
3. Move a step forward if your shot has forced your opponent to the baseline. He may be unable to get sufficient depth from your good length.

Try to trap your opponent into overanticipating certain shots by playing crosscourt or down-the-line shots in a specific pattern. Then play the odd shot for a winner or to draw him away from a particular area. Many players leave the forehand side open and vulnerable in an effort to cover up a weak backhand.

Have a preconceived idea of how much you intend to use crosscourt shots and how to play each opponent. As the game progresses, both players will be trying various plans in hopes of achieving a successful one.

Receiving Serve

Ready Position

Your ready position for return of serve for singles and doubles is a modification of the ready position during a rally.

1. For receiving serve, place your feet comfortably apart with your left foot ahead of the right in a diagonal stance, rather than with your feet side-by-side and parallel. This enables you to have an immediate push forward or backward depending on whether it is a low or high deep serve.
2. It is imperative to be prepared to move forward to smash a poor low serve or to move backward before the high serve gets behind you. Therefore, after taking your position to receive serve, keep your feet stationary until the serve contacts the shuttle.

Receiving

It is important to anticipate the usual direction of the serves and to adjust your position accordingly, shifting your weight in that direction in order to get a faster start.

1. Do not overanticipate. If you do, the server is given the opportunity to surprise you with a change in direction or depth. Take care to keep your percentages in the proper balance.
2. Note in figure 5.2 that the receiver in the right service court is standing closer to the center line than to the sideline in order to protect his or her backhand side. The receiver in the left service court moves toward the backhand side for the same purpose.

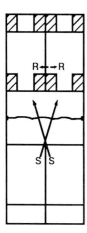

Figure 5.2
Receiving serve in singles.

3. In both cases the receiver is closer to the short service line than to the long service line. This position enables the receiver to attack (hit down) the low serve if it appears but requires more time to move back for the high deep serve.

Common Faults in Receiving Serve

1. Standing too deep in the court, resulting in a defensive (hitting up) return of the low serve.
2. Moving back too slowly, letting the shuttle get behind you.

Whether you are playing singles or doubles, the general rule to follow is to change your position if you are encountering difficulties. Find the place in the court and the position which best suits you and best defies your opponent's plans.

Can you name several good choices for return of a high serve that is falling short?

Singles Strategy

Singles can be described as a "running" game since it requires excellent physical condition to cover the 17' × 22' area. Singles can be a difficult game for some players because it can expose weaknesses that might otherwise be covered up by a partner in doubles play. In general, singles offers the greatest challenge to individual skill and stamina.

The most effective shots in singles play are the high deep serve, the overhead clear (both high and attacking), half-smash, underhand clear, and the hairpin net return. Occasional shots used are the low serve, drive serve, drive, push shot, and the full smash.

Serves

The high deep serve moves the opponent out of center to the back boundary line and thus opens up the front of the court. The low serve used as a change of pace is a method of gaining the offensive since the shuttle may descend as it reaches the top of the net. Therefore, it normally cannot be smashed downward.

Return of Serve

A clear to the opposite baseline is the best and safest return of a deep high serve. If the high serve is short you can hit a dropshot, smash, half-smash, or attacking clear. The offensive can thus be gained with an attacking shot. Choose the shot which you can execute effectively and deceptively.

As in the return of serve, short clears during the rally are disastrous. They can be dealt with more easily and with more variety than shots that fall perpendicular on the back boundary line.

Attack

To attack effectively, remember the following:

1. Force your opponent to play a backhand from deep court.
2. Force your opponent to hit short by using good depth.
3. Hit to the forehand corner in order to open up the backhand side.
4. Meet the shuttle as soon as possible to give your opponent less time.
5. Be deceptive, but it is difficult to be deceptive unless you have plenty of time and are not struggling to reach the shuttle.

Defense

When the opportunity arises for your opponent to play a smash or a dropshot you must defend as well as possible. Return the shuttle close to the net or the baseline as midcourt shots have little value here. Try to use your opponent's speed or angle to your advantage by blocking or guiding the shuttle just over the net with a hairpin net shot. Direct the shuttle to the farthest distance from the attacker.

For example, if your opponent smashes or drops from the deep forehand corner, then you should hit a hairpin net shot to the front backhand corner. If he anticipates the net shot and comes racing in toward the net, flick a flat clear to his backhand corner. Next time go ahead and play the net shot. Alternate your pattern or, better yet, make your pattern random, so your opponent doesn't know what return to expect or just where to expect it.

Types of Singles Play

1. The fast and quick game includes such shots as the low serve, drive serve, flat or attacking clear, drive, and smash.
2. The slower and more deliberate game includes the high serve, high clear, dropshot, and half-smash.

Many players are adept at both fashions of play and the use of a particular one depends on both the opponent and the situation.

Doubles Strategy

Doubles play requires quick racket skill, wit, and cleverness. It is exciting, extremely fast, and demands excellent teamwork. It also requires less stamina than singles and is a game in which weaknesses can be disguised.

The most effective doubles serves include the low serve and flick serve. The most useful doubles shots are the drive, half-smash, smash, and various net returns. This is because a team that hits up often is less likely to win. A team that disciplines itself to hit down consistently can often beat a more physically talented team that hits up with abandon.

Through various maneuvers by the two partners, a player may not have to use his or her less adequate strokes. Instead, both players combine their best assets. Partners unequal in ability can work out a combination that is unusually stable and effective.

Four players, all of different skill levels, can combine and have great fun playing.

Systems of Play

The three systems of doubles play are:

side-by-side (defensive)
up-and-back (attacking)
rotation (a combination of the two)

Men's and womens' doubles teams use all three systems although most prefer rotation. Mixed doubles teams prefer the up-and-back formation.

Side-by-Side or Defensive Formation

A team in a sides formation (S and S) divides the court down the middle from net to back boundary line (fig. 5.3). Each player covers one half of the court, both front and back. The basic serving and receiving positions for the team playing side-by-side place each player in the middle of his or her half of the court.

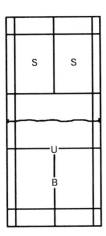

Figure 5.3
Side-by-side and up-and-back doubles formations.

These positions, alterable as the situation changes, are defensive positions. The down-the-middle shots, those directed between the two players, are usually played by the player on the left side since this is that player's forehand side. A team with a left-handed player will discover some interesting advantages and disadvantages, requiring some decisions. It could be agreed that the stronger player is to play the middle shots regardless of which is this player's forehand side.

The advantage of the sides system is that the area which each player is to defend is well-defined and there is little confusion about who is to cover which shots. This defensive side formation is the best system when you have been forced to hit the shuttle upward, thus giving your opponents the opportunity to smash. With both players back from the net, they have more time to defend against the smash and to cover the areas (midcourt and backcourt) where a smash can be directed.

The disadvantage of the system is that the opposite team can play all the shots to one side, up and back, and tire one player. If one player is weaker than the other, the opponents will naturally launch their attack on that player.

Up-and-Back or Offensive Formation

In this system the court is divided in such a way that one player (U) plays the forecourt and the other player (B) plays the backcourt (fig. 5.3). Note the serving (S) and receiving (R) positions for this formation in figure 5.4. The dividing line is about midcourt, depending upon the agreement made by the two partners (P).

The advantage of the up-and-back system lies in the fact that there is always a player at the net to "put away" any loose returns. This keeps the pressure on the opponents.

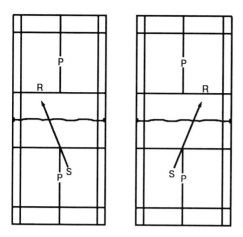

Figure 5.4
Up-and-back doubles formation serving to right and left courts.

For example, as soon as one player can smash or drop from the backcourt, his or her partner moves forward to the net position to cut off any weak returns. Crosscourt shots can be more easily blocked with a player at the net. In addition, this formation makes it easier to protect weaknesses, as each player can cover the part of the court to which his game is best suited.

The disadvantage of the up-and-back system is that the midcourt area along the sidelines is vulnerable. The half-court shot that is played just behind the net player and just in front of the backcourt player tends to cause confusion as to which player is to hit the shuttle. The resulting slight delay may prove disastrous.

Rotation

The rotation system is a means of changing from up-and-back to side-by-side depending on whether a team is attacking or defending.

The attacking team will have to relinquish the up-and-back formation when either player is forced to hit the shuttle upward (defensive). The up-and-back formation is an inadequate defense against the smash because the player at net will not have time to defend and his or her partner cannot protect the entire backcourt against a smash. The net player should backpedal quickly to either side, preferably the closer, and the partner adjusts accordingly. Therefore, when forced on defense, this team reverts to the side-by-side formation until it can regain the attack.

A team on defense can regain the attack by returning smashes with a well-placed halfcourt or drive. The player hitting such a shot should move to the net while the partner pulls around behind him or her, in the up-and-back position, to attack the next shot.

Serves Whatever the system used, the serve is highly important as it gives the opportunity to score. In doubles, the low serve is best and most often used. The flick and drive serves (see chapter 7) are also used effectively as alternatives.

Return of Serve Any high serve should be returned with a smash or overhead dropshot, preferably the smash. However, most of the time the receiver will be low served and has a choice of returning with a drop, drive, or halfcourt. The *drop* should be deceptive, low, and played straight, not crosscourt. The *drive* return is used mostly and ideally has a flat trajectory, and when possible, it is directed to the backhand side although the direction should be varied when necessary. The *halfcourt* is the most difficult to execute as it has to be almost perfect like the drop return or it backfires. It should fall behind the net player at a downward angle in order to force the back player to hit up.

Offense The primary object of the serve, return of serve, and succeeding shots is to force your opponents to hit up thereby giving your side the attack. When this objective is reached, the smash, the half-smash, and overhead dropshot come into play. The smash should win the point outright or force a weak return for the net person to "put away." When smashing, it is very important to be on balance and for the smash to have a sharp downward angle. It should be played to the inside of the opponent who is straight ahead of you or directly down the middle. Crosscourt smash only for variety and to keep both opponents alert. The half-smash is extremely useful to change the pace, particularly after full paced smashes have been used. Overhead dropshots will take less effort and therefore they have their merits. Indiscriminate and nonpurposeful smashing is not intelligent. Mix the overhead drop, smash, and half-smash judiciously and the rewards will be obvious.

Defense Despite all efforts to keep the shuttle going down to maintain the offense, at times your opponents will force you to defend. How good or how bad your opponents are will determine the amount of time you spend defending your court! The smash and dropshot can be returned with a high deep clear, or better yet with a flatter shot at head or shoulder level. The high deep clear keeps you on defense only with the hope of an error by the smasher. The half-court or drive return initiates the turn from defense to offense.

Mixed Doubles Strategy

The systems of doubles play described above are used in men's doubles, women's doubles, and recreational doubles play involving men and women players, with the relative strengths of the players often determining the system and the positions chosen. On the other hand, mixed doubles is a particular event in tournament and club badminton. Traditionally, it is played by the man and woman in an up-and-back formation because, at this level of competition, the speed and the

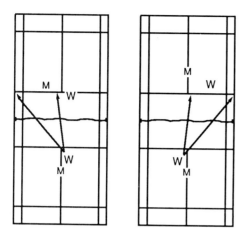

Figure 5.5
Mixed doubles formation—woman serving.

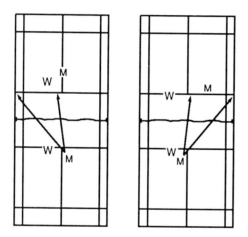

Figure 5.6
Mixed doubles formation—man serving.

smashing power of the man normally exceeds those of the woman. With the up-and-back formation, it is impossible for the man to concentrate his attack on the opposing woman with any degree of success. A more well balanced game results, superior to many games involving men and women.

The strategies below are written with this traditional mixed doubles formation in mind, but they also offer advice to regular doubles teams who elect the up-and-back formation exclusively.

See figures 5.5 and 5.6 for serving and receiving positions.

Which areas of the court are most vulnerable in the up-and-back formation? in the side-by-side formation?

Duties of the Woman (or Front) Player

1. Places shots in the front court and around the short service line.
2. Tries to control the attack by directing the shuttle downward.
3. Uses net and half-court shots to direct shuttle downward.
4. Smashes any "loose" (high and short) shots.
5. Lets clears, fast drives, and smashes pass by to be played by her partner.
6. Rarely moves to the backcourt to play.

Duties of the Man (or Back) Player

1. Plays shots behind and around short service line.
2. Plays half-court shots, drives, and smashes.
3. Plays downward shots that will force a weak return for his partner to "put away."

Use of the Low Serve

1. Keep it low and controlled, normally to inside corner (less angle).
2. Serve to the outside corner occasionally to keep the receiver off balance.
3. Flick serve keeps the receiver off balance and from constantly rushing the low serve.
4. Serve high to the player who is slow moving back or has limited strength overhead.

Return of Serve

1. The half-court shot is the safest and most used. It has moderate speed, falls behind the woman at a downward angle, forcing the man to hit up. Play the halfcourt straight rather than crosscourt most of the time.
2. The dropshot is best used when the woman is serving and should be placed in the alley farthest from her. A drop is risky on the man's serve as his partner is near the net in an attacking position.
3. The drive is pushed or punched faster than the halfcourt and deep in the court. Sometimes a punch directly at the man cramps him and narrows his angle of return as well.

Strategy

1. Use the dropshot and halfcourt to keep the opposing woman guessing and off balance.
2. Use the halfcourt and drive against the opposing man. These shots are best and safest since they are not hit up and they are intended to force an upward return. An upward return invites a smash, and smashes win points.
3. Avoid lifting or hitting the shuttle up.

The rallies often generate into driving duels between two men with the better drive winning. If you concede that the opposing man is excellent at driving, then make more use of the halfcourt and perhaps the drop if the woman is less effective than her partner. It is important for the man to use good judgment when electing to crosscourt a drive by being cognizant of his center position.

Special Defensive Position

Occasions will arise when you will be forced to hit up and defend against a smash. Usually the woman should back up several feet and defend against the crosscourt smash. In this case, she should hold her racket in front of her face for protection as she watches the shuttle and attempts to play it. The man is then responsible for the down-the-line smash and for the dropshot played straight. This net area has now become vulnerable since the woman has backed out and to one side in an effort to return the crosscourt smash.

Normally, the woman plays up in the mixed doubles game. Do you know when it is advisable for her to drop back a few feet?

Conclusion

1. Direct the play to your strengths and to your opponent's weaknesses.
2. Play to your partner's best abilities, cooperate, and discuss your plans.
3. Enjoy the game.

Partners do not enjoy each other if they feel they are not getting to play their own or best shots. The man should not play shots better played by the woman. The woman should play shots that will capitalize on the man's strengths.

In mixed doubles, the woman should let certain shots go past to be played by her partner. Can you name these shots?

Drills and Conditioning

6

The first step in learning badminton, understanding the why and how of stroke development, must be followed by actual stroke practice. No amount of intellectual grasp of the game can substitute for either repetitive practice of the stroke pattern or coordination of the racket and shuttle to assure correct timing. Mental and physical processes should work together to speed up progress.

Badminton is a game requiring great stamina. The shot drills described below are a good start for building the fitness required for badminton, but it is advisable to do more. This chapter also contains suggestions for a conditioning program suited to badminton.

Shot Drills

Various drills and suggestions for individual improvement are given in this chapter. In the diagrams that follow, a solid line (_____) indicates the path of the shuttle, while a broken line (-------) indicates the movement of the players. To make your drills most successful, locate another player with approximately the same degree of skill; neither player benefits sufficiently if the range of skill varies too greatly.

Butterfly Drill

This drill gets its name from the flight pattern of the shuttle (fig. 6.1). It is a good drill to begin with because it does not call for "all-out" hitting or running. Player A serves low to the outside corner of B's service court; B replies with a halfcourt down-the-line. A hits a crosscourt halfcourt, and B again replies with a straight halfcourt. This pattern of halfcourts continues: straight, crosscourt, straight, crosscourt, etc. Players can then reverse roles for balanced practice.

Overhead Clear Drill

Both players take their center positions where the drill for the clear starts with a singles serve and thereafter continues with clears only (fig. 6.2). The clears should first be played parallel to the sideline, then crosscourt, then alternating straight and crosscourt, giving each player a chance to clear from both deep corners. The shuttle should be directed repeatedly to the same corner before changing the direction to the other corner. The player stroking from the backhand should

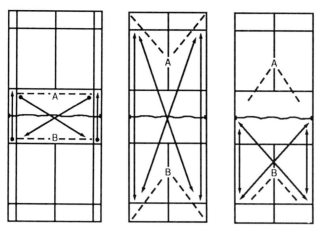

Figure 6.1
Butterfly drill.

Figure 6.2
Overhead clear drill.

Figure 6.3
Overhead dropshot and underhand clear drill.

use an overhead backhand or round-the-head clear. The object is repeatedly to clear the shuttle high and deep from one corner to an opposite corner between the doubles and singles back boundary line. Returning to center position after each hit develops good footwork and stamina.

HINT: Get behind and in line with the shuttle for increased depth. Upon contact, step and move your weight towards the net.

Serve Drill

Perfecting the serve, which is one of the easiest strokes to practice, can be done with or without a partner. To permit the server to take his service position for twenty strokes before retrieving shuttles, about twenty shuttles should be collected. This not only saves time but also adds to the consistency of the stroke. The serve, whether for singles or doubles, should be directed to a particular corner on the court. Practice to all corners for singles and doubles. Even if a partner is present, the serve should not be returned; instead, it should be allowed to fall to the court, enabling the server to see exactly how close to the target the shuttle came.

HINT: Drop the shuttle well away from you in order to get the freedom of movement which will result in better accuracy.

Overhead Dropshot and Underhand Clear Drill

Both players begin in the center position from which the drill starts with a singles serve by A to a back corner (fig. 6.3). The receiver, B, returns it with an overhead dropshot to a front corner. An underhand clear to the same back corner follows and the drill continues: drop, clear, drop, clear; until one player fails to return the shuttle. The shuttle should be directed repeatedly to the same corner until

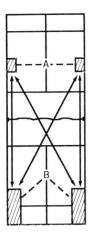

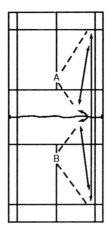

Figure 6.4
Smash and underhand clear drill.

Figure 6.5
Clear-drop-drop drill.

there is some degree of control before switching the direction of the shuttle to another front or back corner. Again, both players should return to the center position if the drill is to simulate game conditions.

HINT: B should pretend to stroke an overhead clear, and A a hairpin net shot, in order to acquire the deception needed for the two shots actually hit.

Smash and Underhand Clear Drill

This drill, very much like the preceding drop and clear drill, begins with a singles serve by A to either back corner (fig. 6.7). The smash by B parallel to the sideline and to the opposite midcourt is returned with a high underhand clear. The drill then becomes—smash, clear, smash, clear; until either player misses; the drill then begins again from center with the serve.

HINT: In order to eliminate faulty shots, start with slower smashes and gradually increase the speed of your smash.

Clear-Drop-Drop Drill

The shots in this drill are all hit straight down-the-line, so two pairs of players can share a court for the drill (fig. 6.4). The three-shot pattern means that roles reverse each cycle in the drill. A clears high to B, B hits an overhead drop, and A responds with a net drop. Here the roles reverse: B runs in to hit a clear (underhand), A hits an overhead drop, and B hits a net drop. The drill continues as it started with A hitting a clear.

Clear-Smash-Drop Drill

This drill is very similar to the clear-drop-drop drill above. Instead of hitting an overhead drop off the clear, B hits a straight smash instead, and A responds with an underhand drop. The pattern continues with B clearing so that A can smash.

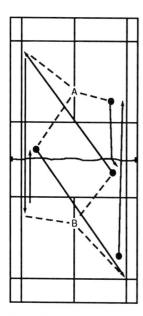

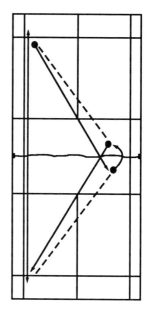

Figure 6.6
Running smash drill.

Figure 6.7
Four clear-two drop drill.

Running Smash

This drill is a simple variation of the clear-smash-drop drill above, and it requires the entire court (fig. 6.5). The shot pattern is still clear-smash-drop, but while the smash and drop are hit straight, the clear is hit crosscourt. This drill is particularly good practice for the round-the-head smash.

Four Clear-Two Drop Drill

This drill also requires the entire court and has a six-shot pattern: four straight clears, one overhead crosscourt drop, one straight net drop (fig. 6.6). A clears to B in one deep corner, B clears, A clears, and B clears, all straight. Then, A hits a crosscourt drop, which B runs in to return with a net drop straight. A runs in to clear out of B's deep corner, starting the next cycle.

Drive Drill

There are four drives to be practiced: the straight (parallel to the sideline) forehand and backhand, and the crosscourt forehand and backhand (fig. 6.8). This drill begins with both players in the center of the court. One player hits a drive serve to the predetermined forehand or backhand of the opponent. Thereafter, repeated drives ensue: forehand to forehand; backhand to backhand; forehand to

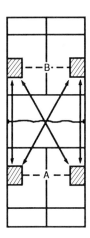

Figure 6.8
Drive drill.

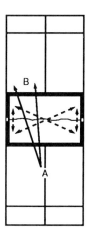

Figure 6.9
Short game.

backhand; and backhand to forehand. Each of the four strokes should be practiced repeatedly before the side and direction are changed. Little backswing should be used for these drives; punch the shuttle with a quick wrist motion. Return to center after each hit.

HINT: Contact the drive high so that this drill does not become a smash, clear drill.

Short Game

This game, played and scored exactly according to singles rules, begins with a low serve by A and return of serve at the net by B: thereafter, only net shots, straight or crosscourt, can be played (fig. 6.9). Any shots, other than the serve, which fall behind the short service line are considered out of court. This drill, valuable to beginners learning rules and scoring, develops the skill and judgment in the forecourt necessary in doubles and mixed doubles.

HINT: Stand far enough away from the net to give yourself time and space to stroke properly.

Three Stroke Drill

The first three shots of a point, important because the offense or defense may easily be determined with initial shots, should be practiced in that order and a decision made after each sequence as to the effectiveness of the serve, return of serve, and the third shot.

HINT: Try to be in an offensive position after the third shot.

Endurance Conditioning

Whether a player is able to finish the match or practice period in good fashion, that is, still stroking the shuttle with power and control, is determined largely by physical condition. The player in poor condition begins to make errors and to be slow afoot after a short period of time. Badminton should be a game of long, interesting rallies free from outright errors, and this demands strength and endurance.

There are various ways of improving one's endurance. Distance running, soccer, hockey, basketball—in fact, all the running games—are of value. Modern dance, gymnastics, and rope skipping add quickness and flexibility. Tennis, racketball, and squash, closely related to badminton, require some strokes similar to the badminton player's game. Care must be given, however, not to adopt the firm wrist and longer backswings of these other racket sports. Table tennis is excellent for improving reflexes. All these activities contribute to the conditioning process, but obviously the best conditioning for badminton is to play badminton. If the stroke practice drills are rehearsed properly with each player returning to center position between each stroke, endurance will be developed. Practice games against someone of exact equal ability will result in long, endurance-demanding rallies.

Needless to say, tobacco and alcohol negatively affect one's physical condition. Adequate sleep and food supply the energy reserve needed to meet the demands of a strenuous game.

Here are several on-court drills which are very effective in building fitness for badminton.

Clear-Tap Drill

This drill is effective in developing stamina for long rallies, and two pairs can share the court. The drill consists entirely of overhead clears, but in between hitting clears, each player must run in to tap his or her racket on the short service line. Players quickly find that it pays both to be moving forward as they clear and to hit the clears sufficiently high and deep.

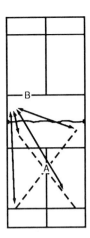

Figure 6.10
Unequal partner drill.

Unequal Partner Drill

Many times good players unable to find opponents of like skill can devise ways of utilizing beginners as practice partners (fig. 6.10). For instance, the advanced player (A) strokes the shuttle to one corner of the court to the beginner (B) who may then return the shuttle any place on the court. The advanced player develops control by playing the shuttle to the beginner's racket, thus enabling him to keep the rally going. The advanced player develops footwork, stamina, and stroke control chasing the comparatively uncontrolled returns of the novice. This drill can be amusing and fun to two players desiring to learn (each at his own level) and willing to cooperate.

HINT: Enjoy the practice as if it were a game.

Techniques for Better Players

7

It is fun to experiment with additional strokes and shots to use in combination with the essential skills described in chapters 3 and 4. Descriptions of advanced techniques, such as the round-the-head and high backhand strokes, varieties of serves, forms of deception, and more advanced net play, will be found in this chapter. Many of these strokes are no more difficult to execute than the basic ones, but they consist of refinements and variations that are easier to learn once the basic strokes are mastered. Dwelling too soon on spectacular shots, at the expense of the standard ones used most of the time, tends to be discouraging and counterproductive.

Nevertheless, as you gain experience and perfect your basic strokes, you will want to add threat to your game. The fact that your opponent must be alert to this possibility further assures the effectiveness of the basic strokes. In this chapter, you will learn how to carry out the following:

the round-the-head stroke
the high backhand stroke
the flick serve
the drive serve
the backhand serve
"holding" the shuttle
the net flick
the push shot
the net smash.

Advanced Strokes and Shots

The Round-the-Head Stroke

The round-the-head stroke is an overhead forehand stroke, but it is an unusual one because the shuttle is contacted on the left or backhand side of the body. This stroke may be used to produce a clear, a dropshot, or a smash. The execution of this stroke is similar to that of the normal overhead forehand (see chapter 4 for instructions), but there are differences in footwork and in the path of the racket swing that are described in the following section.

Figure 7.1
Round-the-head stroke.

Procedure

1. The major difference from the normal overhead stroke is that the contact point is above your left shoulder, necessitating a reach to the left and a leaning of the body.
2. The stroke is played with your body facing the net and either with the weight on the left foot (fig. 7.1) or with the body in the air (fig. 7.2).
3. The right leg and body weight swing forward to the follow-through. If the stroke is taken with the body in the air, the legs execute a "scissors" action as the right leg swings forward and the left leg plants on the court after the shot to push back to center.

Strategy

Many sound reasons exist for taking the shuttle with a round-the-head stroke rather than with a backhand stroke. First, more power and deception are usually possible on the round-the-head than on the backhand. This in turn means more depth and speed on the shuttle, and hence a more effective shot will be produced. In addition, since the opponent will often be attacking the backhand corner, it is imperative that this area be protected at every opportunity. The round-the-head stroke meets this need. For example, if an attacking clear or drive serve to the backhand can be anticipated, the shuttle can be intercepted in front of the body and hit more quickly with a round-the-head shot.

Bruce Hazelton/Focus West

Louis Ross

Figure 7.2
Round-the-head stroke.

Figure 7.3
High backhand stroke.

The results of this stroke are not always favorable, however, as the feet and body have to be moved to the left side of the court and a large portion of the forehand side of the court is left open. Advantages gained by the round-the-head, such as a stronger shot, will have to be weighed against the disadvantages. The strength of your backhand and your speed of foot will be determining factors in selecting the round-the-head instead of the backhand. The ideal player will be able to play the high backhand stroke as well as the round-the-head.

Why might one choose to use a round-the-head stroke? What are the advantages and disadvantages?

The High Backhand Stroke

Many players believe that the high backhand stroke, particularly one used to produce a clear shot from deep court, is the most difficult stroke in badminton. This is not necessarily the case, especially given the light rackets available today. If you follow the procedures below, you will be able to hit clears, dropshots, and even smashes with the high backhand. The most important thing to remember is that, contrary to all other shots, the high backhand is best hit with the shuttle slightly behind your body and with your back partly turned towards the net (fig. 7.3).

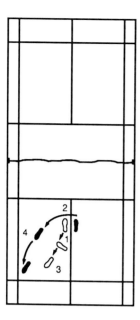

Figure 7.4
Footwork to deep backhand corner.

Procedure

1. Use the backhand grip, with the ball of the thumb flat against the back bevel of the handle, as described for the backhand drive.
2. Follow the footwork in figure 7.4 to move to the deep left corner. Your right foot should be out front, pointing to the side or back corner, with your back turned partially to the net.
3. At the completion of the backswing, the racket should be well back behind your body with the right elbow pointing up at the shuttle.
4. The most important aspect of the swing for the clear is the timing of the wrist and forearm as they unfold and swing the head of the racket up to meet the shuttle above and just behind the right shoulder. Rather than pulling your whole arm through in a broad stroke, stop your wrist at the highest point, and let the racket whip through in a tight circle centered at your wrist. If you have pulled the racket up to that point with a hard early swing, the racket head will whip through at a great velocity (fig. 7.5).
5. If the angle of the racket face is upwards at the point of contact, you will hit a deep clear. If the angle is down, you will hit a smash. To hit a dropshot, do not let the racket head whip through, but instead guide the shuttle to the net with a slower forearm motion.
6. As you hit the high backhand, your trunk and shoulders will naturally rotate back towards the net as you return to center.

Figure 7.5
High backhand stroke.

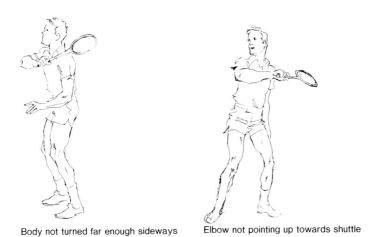

Body not turned far enough sideways   Elbow not pointing up towards shuttle

Figure 7.6
Mistakes most commonly made with the high backhand stroke.

Strategy

Excellent timing and power are essential on the high backhand to clear the shuttle high enough and deep enough to make it a safe shot. A deep shot to your left side can be played instead with a round-the-head shot, but your court position would be sacrificed. If you can develop both an accurate drop and a decent clear off the high backhand, you can thereby prevent an opponent from taking advantage of you on that side. A player must assess his own capabilities before selecting the particular shots to use.

In what important way does the high backhand stroke violate the general principles of effective stroking?

How is a deep clear produced from the high backhand stroke? from a dropshot? from a smash?

The Flick Serve

The flick serve is a high serve used almost exclusively in doubles. It is a deceptive alternative to the low serve designed to keep the opponent from rushing your low serve. It will often produce a weak return which can be easily killed. Occasionally it will produce an ace.

Procedure

1. In delivering the serve in doubles, always start with your wrist cocked back at almost a right angle.
2. To deliver a low serve, merely guide the shuttle over the net with a pushing motion of the arm, using the wrist hardly at all.
3. If you expect the opponent to rush the serve, deliver a flick serve by snapping the wrist through at the last moment, sending the shuttle just over the opponent's racket to a point just inside the long doubles service line. (See figure 7.7 for the flight path.)
4. Be careful not to use any preliminary faking motions; these are not legal on the serve. Simply make the two serves look the same until the last moment. Be careful also not to commit a service fault; contact the shuttle *below* your waist and with your hand *above* the racket head.

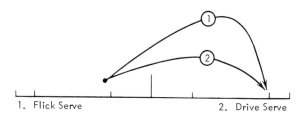

1. Flick Serve   2. Drive Serve

Figure 7.7
Flight patterns of advanced serves in doubles.

The Drive Serve

The drive serve is another alternative to the low serve in doubles and can also be useful in singles. Its trajectory is quite flat, like the drive, and should cramp the receiver by coming into his body quickly (fig. 7.7).

Elements of the Drive Serve

1. The weak return is the desired outcome of a good drive serve.
2. Sheer speed and force of shot will not be enough for success.
3. Very few points are won outright on the drive serve, or on any serve, since it is played from an underhand (defensive) position.
4. If the drive serve can jolt your opponent off balance and thus place you in an offensive position, the immediate objective has been achieved.
5. The mistake made by an ambitious receiver upon returning a good drive serve is to try to do too much with it. If the shuttle has carried behind the receiver as the server has planned it, the receiver should be content to play a safe, high, deep clear in order to regain balance. This serve will not be so effective if your opponent's speed of reflexes is exceptionally good.
6. Against a player of different capabilities or against a player whose court position is faulty, the drive serve may be the answer to a serving problem.

Strategy

The drive serve, most frequently used in doubles, has a specific value to a side-by-side (defensive) team. The angle that can be attained by serving from a position near the sideline can make an aggressive return almost impossible.

In conclusion, the effectiveness of the drive serve is due to its angle, speed, and some degree of deception. It must be noted here that the deception must be in the wrist. Any preliminary movements of the body intended to fool the receiver are illegal on the serve. If the server delays hitting the shuttle for so long as to be unfair to the receiver, it is a fault. This faulty tactic is called a balk.

The Backhand Serve

This serve was developed primarily by Asian players and is now used by many players throughout the world. For a few years, it was used to strike the feathers first with a cutting motion that made the shuttle swerve in flight. The Laws now require the base of the shuttle to be hit first on the serve, but the backhand serve can still be effective.

Procedure (See figure 7.8)

1. Stand square to the net with your feet side-by-side, or place the right foot slightly forward.
2. Using a backhand grip, shortened to give more control, hold the racket below your waist and just touching your body.

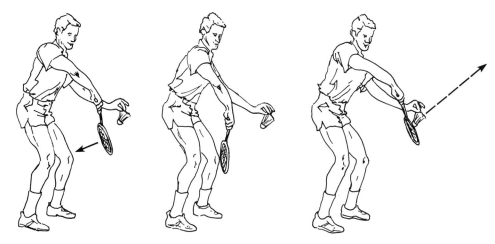

Figure 7.8
Backhand serve.

3. Hold the shuttle by the tips of several feathers in front of your body, with the base pointed toward the racket.
4. Bring the racket forward to stroke the shuttle gently over the net towards the opponent's short service line.
5. If your opponent is rushing the serve too often, you can occasionally use the flick or drive serve on the backhand for a surprise.

Strategy

The backhand serve is a useful service variation because:
1. The shuttle is hit in front of the body and takes very little time to reach its destination.
2. The shuttle is hard to see against the server's clothes if they are white.

What are the advantages of the half-smash over the smash, and the backhand short serve over the forehand short serve?

"Holding" the Shuttle

Objective

The objective of all underhand shots, other than the serve, is to distract the opponent with deceptive moves. A phrase used often by badminton players, "holding the shuttle," refers to pretending to hit the shuttle before you actually do. For example, if when you pretend to play a dropshot, your opponent moves toward the net and you then flick the shuttle to the backcourt; you have "held the shot." This type of deception is generally employed with underhand shots. Deception on overhead shots results from preparing to stroke each shot identically as described in chapter 4.

Procedure

1. You may hold the shot by a feint of the racket, head, or body. It takes time, however, to be deceptive.
2. If you are running at full speed to return the shuttle, there is not time to produce feints! When you find the pace is slower and you have the time, reach forward to play the shuttle; then let it drop and contact it at a lower point.
3. During the time the shuttle is dropping, your opponent may be committing himself forward or back. Be alert to this and either drop or flick the shuttle accordingly.
4. If your opponent is moving too soon and getting caught repeatedly, he will be forced to hold his position until you actually contact the shuttle.
5. Continue to watch the shuttle closely. You will tend to take your eye off the shuttle in order to see if and in which direction your opponent is moving.

If your errors tell you that you are mis-hitting and indulging in needless fancy racket work, go back to the basics. If you can master this deception, however, it is a tremendous weapon against a player who is very fleet of foot or likes to play a fast game. Slow the game down with defensive shots and then put your deception to work. Hopefully he will tire as a result; then you can apply your pace and power attack.

Advanced Net Shots and Play

In chapter 4, the hairpin net shot was described. There are several other net shots that can be effective when hit from the same position, especially when deceptive techniques such as "holding" the shuttle are employed. These are the net flick, the push shot, and the net smash.

The Net Flick

This shot is a valuable alternative to the hairpin drop, especially in singles. It is played at or just below the net level, and the beginning of the stroke should lead the opponent to believe that a hairpin drop is coming. Get to the shuttle early, and reach out to it with the racket head cocked back; in this way, you are "holding" the shuttle. At the last moment, snap your wrist through and send the shuttle to the baseline. See figure 7.9 for the best trajectory.

The net flick is particularly effective with an opponent who tends to over-anticipate and rush the net after hitting a drop.

The Push Shot

The push shot is just what the name implies—a push, not a stroke. It is played at or above net level with the head of the racket up and the face of the racket flat. Its direction is angled downward. Refer to figure 7.9.

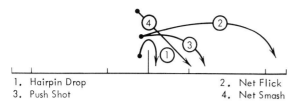

1. Hairpin Drop   2. Net Flick
3. Push Shot   4. Net Smash

Figure 7.9
Flight patterns produced by net shots.

The use of the push shot, almost nonexistent in singles, becomes highly effective in doubles. When a doubles team takes an up-and-back formation, the shot should be pushed down with a medium amount of speed to the opponent's midcourt. This will place the shuttle just behind the net player and force the backcourt player to reach and stroke the shuttle up. Confusion often results as to which player should return this shot. Obviously, the push shot cannot be played from below net level.

The Net Smash

The other highly important net shot that has to be played above net level is the smash. The shot is accomplished by a downward snap of the wrist. It is the best return of a high, short shot. It is the kill! Care must be taken not to get excessively enthusiastic at the prospect of a setup and bang the shuttle or your racket into the net. Instead, keep your eye on the shuttle and control your swing until the point is completed. The direction of the smash at this close range is not important. If directed straight to the floor with great speed, the smash will be unreturnable (fig. 7.9).

Strokes and Strategy

Using the strokes described in chapters 4 and 7 in an appropriate sequence, you must outthink your opponent. Preconceived strategy and play are fine until you meet your equal or your supposed superior, in which case your thinking must be spontaneous. Your shots must have speed and control, and the decision as to the pattern or order they take must be made in the fury of the game. In singles, perhaps it will be two clears and then the drop, or clear and drop, and drop again; in doubles, a push shot, a smash, and another smash. In either game catch your opponent going the wrong way by not playing to the obvious open space; because he has moved to that obvious space, play behind him. Sometimes you may be caught in your own trap, but if your percentage of "catching" is greater than your percentage of being "caught," then you are ahead of the game.

If your strokes are well executed and the rallies are long and the play interesting and close, then consider your game successful. That's the fun of the game. Mastery of the strokes will make it possible for you to delight in meeting a contemporary and pitting your forces against his. Play with enthusiasm and enjoyment. The winning and the rewards, whatever they may be, will be forthcoming. Reaching this stage of enjoyment comes as a result of concentrated practice.

In doubles, what is the prime factor determining your choice of shot while you are playing in the "up" position? How does the execution of a smash from this position differ from a smash taken from midcourt?

Badminton—A Short History

" . . . to play shuttlecock methinks is the game now . . ."
Two Maids of Moreclacke (Anon), 1609

Devotees of sports take pride in tracing the roots of their games as far back into the past as possible. In this search, few sports can match badminton, for its roots are clearly established in civilizations which flourished over 2000 years ago, and its development is chronicled century by century down to the present.

Ancient Times

The shuttlecock, badminton's unique object, was central to the ancient Chinese game of *Ti Jian Zi,* or shuttlecock kicking. Evidence of this game dates back at least to the 1st century B.C. Shuttlecock kicking was also popular in the neighboring areas of Japan, India, and Siam, and soon found its way to Sumeria and Greece. Although the shuttle was usually hit by feet or hands, various bats were occasionally used as well.

Exactly how and why the shuttlecock's popularity became so widespread so early is not clear. It is reasonable to assume, however, that feathers from eaten fowl were plentiful and that perhaps methods of storing them, such as sticking them into cork or balls of yarn, led to the discovery of a delightful plaything. The fascination and enjoyment of striking a shuttlecock back and forth, either in gentle play or in fierce competition, is a thread running through the ages.

Medieval Times and 17th Century

English woodcut illustrations from the 14th and 15th centuries show peasants batting a shuttlecock to each other with rectangular wooden paddles, and by late in the 16th century this had become a popular children's game. The word "battledore" was given to the striking instrument, being a derivative of the Old English word *batt,* for cudgel. William Shakespeare makes reference to battledore and shuttlecock many times in his plays and other writings. Samuel Pepys in his *Diary* makes reference to "shittlecock."

The social status of battledore-shuttlecock rose in the 17th century, as it became a pastime for royalty and the leisured classes. As such, in France, it was called *jeu de volant,* or "game of shuttlecock." A 1638 etching from the French court shows a fine gentleman volleying a shuttle by himself with a well strung battledore in each hand. The Parisian artist Jean Chardin painted a masterpiece "Jeune Fille Jouant au Volant" (Young Girl Playing at Shuttlecock) which now hangs in Florence's famous Uffizi Gallery.

Prince Henry, son of King James I of England, is said to have been "playing at shuttle-cocke with one farr taller than himself and hittyng him by chance with the shuttlecocke upon the forehead." This quotation from *Two Maids of Moreclacke* suggests that even as early as the 1600s there was an element of real competition in the playing of the game.

In Germany and Scandinavia the game became known as *federball,* or featherball, and in 1650 Queen Kristina of Sweden built a special court for herself and visiting noblemen near Stockholm's Royal Palace. Even Catherine the Great is said to have played in Russia.

At this patrician level, the shuttle was hit into play at the start of a rally by a servant, hence the term, "to serve."

18th Century

Battledore and shuttlecock was an accepted institution in Europe in the 1700s. The French author de Garsault devoted six paragraphs to the shuttlecock in a book on the *Art of the Tennis Racket Maker,* and he lamented the age-old problem that shuttles cost too much and were "quickly spoiled." Art continued to record the game's popularity. In Poland, Adam Manyoki painted "Young Prince Sulkowski" with a shuttle and battledore, and an English portrait (c. 1740) of the young Earl of Dysart depicts him similarly.

The first evidence of battledore-shuttlecock in America dates to this period. The popularity of the game in England during King James' time certainly caused it to spread to the colonies, but exactly when is not known. Yet, in 1742, the London merchant wrote Mrs. Ross of Annapolis, "You sent for shuttlecocks and no battledores, whether you intended to omit them I could not guess, but as they are used together, I sent them so, with variety, I hope 'tis not wrong." A 1766 advertisement in New York by one James Rivington stated that he sold battledores and shuttlecocks. A 1790 tapestry from colonial Williamsburg shows two boys hitting a shuttlecock back and forth on a Virginia hillside.

Throughout this time, the game appears to have been especially popular with young people, but the object of the game was still primarily to hit the shuttle *to* each other, or to oneself, and to keep it in the air as long as possible. The idea of a net and of trying to prevent one's partner from returning the shuttle was still a century away.

The term "to serve" is common to several sports. What is the origin of the term?

A French author in the 1700s wrote about problems with shuttlecocks that are still experienced by today's players. What were the difficulties?

19th Century

By the early 1800s, battledore and shuttlecock was a regular fixture in English country houses. These country gentlemen were sportsmen; and one in particular, the 7th Duke of Beaufort, issued a series of books on sports and games named after his Gloucestershire estate, Badminton House. His family, the Somersets, were avid players at shuttlecock: inscriptions on the vellum heads of their battledores record rallies consisting of 2,117 shots on January 12, 1830, and of 2,018 shots in February, 1845.

The transition from battledore-shuttlecock to badminton, building slowly for over 1800 years, quickened in the 1850s and 1860s. One day, someone stretched a string across the middle of the Front Hall at Badminton House, making an elementary net. Whether it was the Somerset children, or one of the Duke's sporting friends, or a visiting Army officer who had seen such a net in India, no one can be certain. In any case, the "new game" *badminton battledore* was advertised by a London toy dealer in 1860, and by 1867 a rather formal game, with lines and real nets, was being played in India by English officers and their families. Although the precise birthplace and birthdate of modern badminton is thus impossible to specify, it is certain that the latter took place before the March 1874 inauguration of modern lawn tennis.

From 1870 to 1900, badminton came of age as a competitive indoor sport. The first rules appeared in India in 1873, and clubs were formed throughout the British Isles to promote competition. The first tournaments were held there early in the 1890s, and the first All-England Championships were held in 1899. Until the 1920s, the major titles were contested by English, Scots, and Irish. Rules varied from place to place until about 1905, when the Badminton Association of England adopted and promulgated uniform new rules which are in essence those followed today.

The Modern Game

Beginning in the 1920s, badminton spread first to northern Europe, becoming especially popular in the Scandinavian countries, and then to North America and the Far East. The Irishman who had dominated the All-Englands in the early 1920s, Frank Devlin, was instrumental in promoting the game in Canada, and the interest in badminton developed by the British in India and Malaya was soon found throughout Asia, as one country after another rose to the top ranks: Thailand and Indonesia in the 1950s, Japan in the 1960s, China in the 1970s, and Korea in the 1980s.

The International Badminton Federation was formed in 1934 with nine member countries and grew to the more than 85 nations currently affiliated in the 1980s. Various international competitions for teams and individuals were instituted in the post-war years—see chapter 9—and by 1979 the game had become fully professional. A year-long circuit of open tournaments throughout the world attracted the top players to a touring career similar to that of other professional athletes. The decision in 1985 to make badminton an Olympic sport solidified the game's position as a major international sport for all time.

Badminton in the United States

In 1878, two New Yorkers—Bayard Clarke and E. Langdon Wilks—returned from overseas trips to India and England, respectively, having been exposed to badminton on their travels. With a friend, Oakley Rhinelander, they formed the

Badminton Club of the City of New York, the oldest badminton club in the world in continuous existence. Badminton was primarily a society game for New York's upper crust until 1915, when intercity competitions with Boston's Badminton Club, formed in 1908, created a serious rivalry that continued through the 1920s.

By 1930, the game was spreading across the country and had become a serious, demanding sport for women and men alike. Clubs mushroomed on the Eastern seaboard, in the Midwest, and on the Pacific Coast. The Hollywood movie colony took to the game eagerly, under the encouragement of a touring professional, George "Jess" Willard, who played exhibitions in movie houses across the country to packed houses and thereby did much to bring the game to the American people. Willard was followed on the national circuit by Ken Davidson, a Scotsman whose badminton comedy routines entertained millions in exhibitions in the 1930's and 1940's, and by Davidson's early partner, Hugh Forgie, a Canadian whose badminton-on-ice shows became world famous in the 1950's and 1960's. These three men combined great badminton talent with superb showmanship to spread the game in the United States and worldwide.

Through the leadership of some of Boston's leading players, the American Badminton Asssociation was formed in 1936, and the first national championships were held in 1937 in Chicago. One of the most famous names in world badminton appeared at the 1939 championships held in New York. An 18-year-old Pasadenan, David G. Freeman, upset the defending champion Walter Kramer in the men's singles final to begin a winning streak that would last his 10-year badminton career. In 1949 he won the U.S. Championship, the All-England Championship, and all his matches in the first Thomas Cup competitions. He then retired to continue his career as neurosurgeon, and he is still considered perhaps the finest player the game has seen.

Following World War II, the first national junior championships were held in 1947, and the development of badminton in schools and colleges led to the first national collegiate championships in 1970. The United States men's team made the Thomas Cup final rounds throughout the 1950s, and the women's team held the Uber Cup from 1957 until 1966; but the rapid development of the game across the world soon left the United States behind. Badminton continued to grow in the United States but at a much slower pace than during the pre-war years. Golf, tennis, and the major professional sports came to the fore, while the popular misconception of badminton as only a leisurely recreation proved difficult to overcome. With the addition of badminton to the Olympic Games as of 1992, it seems only a matter of time before the game will once again become a sport of great national popularity and recognition.

For more complete histories of badminton and for reproductions of the interesting drawings and paintings mentioned above, the reader is referred to the books by Bernard Adams and Pat Davis listed in the Appendix.

Facts for Competitors

9

United States Badminton Association

The governing body for badminton in the United States is the United States Badminton Association (USBA). Through its regional and state associations and member clubs, the USBA administers competitive badminton play and promotes the development of badminton in this country. The Board of Directors of the USBA establishes national policies for badminton, and the USBA office is responsible for the day-to-day administration of national badminton activity.

United States Badminton Association
501 West Sixth Street
Papillion, NE 68046
(402) 592–7309

The USBA was founded as the American Badminton Association in 1936, and the current name was adopted in 1978. The general purposes of the USBA are these:

1. Promotion and development of badminton play and competition in the United States, without monetary gain.
2. Establishment and upholding of the Laws of Badminton, as adopted by the International Badminton Federation.
3. Arrangement and oversight of the various United States National and Open Championship tournaments.
4. Sanctioning of other tournaments at the local, state, and regional level.
5. Selection and management of players and teams representing the United States in international competitions, including the Olympic Games and the Pan American Games.
6. Representation of the United States and of the USBA's interests in activities and decisions of the International Badminton Federation and the United States Olympic Committee.

The USBA is well worth joining because of these purposes and the many services provided to badminton players at all levels. Some of these services are listed below; further information can be obtained from the national office.

Membership

Membership in the USBA is required for participation in USBA sanctioned tournaments and for the right to be considered for national ranking and international competition. There are various categories of membership: Life, Regular, Junior, Club, and Institution. Life membership is granted to those individuals making a one-time contribution of $500 to the USBA, a nonprofit institution incorporated in Louisiana; other members pay an annual fee. Life and Regular members may vote and sanction tournaments; all members receive USBA publications.

The Club and Institution categories are group memberships. Each such group receives one vote (in the group name), all USBA publications, and the right to sanction tournaments. Tournament and ranking privileges do not accrue to players in such groups unless they join the USBA individually.

National Magazine

The USBA national magazine, *Badminton USA,* is published five times per year. It provides articles of interest to club and tournament players, as well as national rankings and tournament schedules and results. All USBA members receive *Badminton USA,* but additional subscriptions may be obtained through the national office.

Handbook—Rules Book

One of the USBA's most important functions is its responsibility for establishing the rules under which badminton is played in the United States. It therefore publishes the "Official Rules of Play," as part of its official Handbook. This is available from the national office at a reasonable price.

Video Library

The USBA maintains an extensive library of badminton videofilms. Many of these show tournament competition between national and world champions; others offer series of badminton instruction. These cassettes, available in VHS or Beta format, may be rented at reasonable rates.

Equipment

Although the USBA does not sell badminton equipment, other than a small selection of pins, shirts, and sweat clothes, the national office will provide a list of badminton equipment suppliers on request.

Clubs and Contacts

One publication particularly useful to traveling players is a listing of badminton clubs and contact persons, by zip code, throughout the United States. This list, along with information about badminton play in a particular area, may be obtained from the national office.

Education Foundation

The USBA is aided in its efforts by the United States Badminton Education Foundation (USBEF), established to attract and build endowment support for badminton development programs in this country. Information about the USBEF and how to make gifts to it are available from the USBA office.

Badminton Camps

For those who wish to obtain expert instruction over an extended period, participation in one of a number of badminton camps is suggested. These camps provide work on strokes, footwork, and conditioning, with the use of video instruction, evaluation, drills, and practice. Also included are informal play with other groups and coaches, suggestions for diet and for care and prevention of athletic injuries, and coaching ideas for large groups. Contact the USBA office for camp information.

Portable Badminton Courts

Several companies, notably Supreme All-Weather Surfaces (Cartersville, GA) and Bolltex (Tennis Surfaces Co., Wheaton, IL), manufacture portable badminton surfaces. These may be laid out in any gymnasium, hall, or other high-ceilinged room where the floor surface is unsuitable for badminton play. The overall size of each court is about 50' × 25' in one or several pieces which may be rolled up and stored. The courts are lined and ready for play and may be obtained with nets and posts and a dolly for handling.

Tournament Sanctions

Tournaments may be sanctioned by obtaining a sanction form from the USBA office, filling it out, and returning it with a sanction fee. The USBA office will provide with the sanction certificate a full packet of information and advice on the running of a successful tournament.

School Tournaments

The USBA gives special consideration to schools and colleges regarding sanction fees and membership requirements for tournaments held for students. Contact the USBA office for details.

Tournaments

Many indoor tournaments are available to those who like real competition. Tournaments are held on various levels: club, school, city, state, regional, intercollegiate, national, and international. Events normally offered are men's singles, women's singles, men's doubles, women's doubles, and mixed doubles. These are held for juniors at various age levels (Under 12, 14, 16, and 18), for adults, and for seniors at various age levels (35, 45, 55, and 65 and Over). Many areas classify players into flights designated "A," "B," and "C," so that players compete with others close to their ability; some areas also hold novice tournaments regularly to encourage beginners to compete.

Information regarding dates and locations of tournaments may be found in *Badminton USA,* as well as in badminton newsletters published by local associations. The United States National Championships (junior, adult, and senior) are held annually in the spring—March or April. The United States Open Championships, attracting players from around the world, are held each year in the fall, October or November as part of a North American circuit of tournaments including Canada and Mexico.

The oldest and most famous tournament in the world is the All-England Championship, played in London every March. It was first held in 1899 and attracts hundreds of entrants from around the world. So large and talented is the entry, in fact, that the qualifying tournament held the week prior is itself the size of the All-England and is as difficult a tournament as many international open tournaments.

International Badminton Federation

The International Badminton Federation (IBF) governs international badminton competition throughout the world. The IBF was founded in 1934 as an outgrowth of the Badminton Association (of England), which had governed play since 1893. The United States joined in 1938 and has participated actively in all IBF-sponsored competitions since that time.

World Badminton is the official publication of the IBF. It contains reports on major tournaments and team competitions held around the world, as well as articles of general interest about badminton. The photographs of top players in action make this publication especially worthwhile.

International Badminton Federation
24 Winchcombe House, Winchcombe Street
Cheltenham, Gloucestershire
England GL52 2NA

The IBF sponsors four major international competitions:

Thomas Cup—International Men's Team Championship
Uber Cup—International Ladies' Team Championship
World Championships—Individual Competition
Sudirman Cup—World Mixed Team Championship

It is the dream of every young player to represent the United States in one of these events.

Thomas Cup

The Thomas Cup was donated to the IBF in 1939 by Sir George Thomas, one of England's leading badminton and chess players of the early 1900s. His purpose was to create for badminton a competition similar to the Davis Cup in tennis. The competition was delayed by World War II until 1949 and was held triennially for many years, until the decision was made after the 1982 contest to hold the event every two years and to reduce the number of matches in a nation-vs.-nation "tie" from nine to five. Results of the final rounds to date are as follows:

1948–49 Malaya defeated Denmark, 8–1
1951–52 Malaya defeated USA, 7–2
1954–55 Malaya defeated Denmark, 8–1
1957–58 Indonesia defeated Malaya, 6–3
1960–61 Indonesia defeated Thailand, 6–3
1963–64 Indonesia defeated Denmark, 5–4
1966–67 Malaysia defeated Indonesia, 6–3
1969–70 Indonesia defeated Malaysia, 6–2
1972–73 Indonesia defeated Denmark, 8–1
1975–76 Indonesia defeated Malaysia, 9–0
1978–79 Indonesia defeated Denmark, 9–0
1981–82 China defeated Indonesia, 5–4
1984   Indonesia defeated China, 3–2
1986   China defeated Indonesia, 3–2
1988   China defeated Malaysia, 4–1

Uber Cup

The Ladies' International Championship for the Uber Cup was begun in 1957 with a team trophy donated by one of England's greatest players, Mrs. H. S. (Betty) Uber. Also once held triennially in separate years from the Thomas Cup, the Uber Cup is now contested every two years concurrently with the Thomas Cup. Results of the final rounds to date are as follows:

1956–57 United States defeated Denmark, 6–1
1959–60 United States defeated Denmark, 5–2
1962–63 United States defeated England, 4–3
1965–66 Japan defeated United States, 5–2
1968–69 Japan defeated Indonesia, 6–1
1971–72 Japan defeated Indonesia, 6–1
1974–75 Indonesia defeated Japan, 5–2
1977–78 Japan defeated Indonesia, 5–2
1981–82 Japan defeated Indonesia, 6–3
1984   China defeated England, 5–0
1986   China defeated Indonesia, 5–0
1988   China defeated Korea, 5–0

The competitions for the Thomas and Uber Cups are now held during even-numbered years, and each tie consists of three singles and two doubles matches. Regional playoffs are held in February in several locations around the world, and the winners of these playoffs along with the defending nations gather in one location in May or June for the final rounds.

World Championships

The World Badminton Championships were initiated in 1977 to provide individual championships complementing the team competitions described above. They are now held in odd-numbered years, alternating with the Cup contests, at sites which vary:

1977—Stockholm
1980—Djakarta
1983—Copenhagen
1985—Calgary
1987—Beijing
1989—Djakarta

Sudirman Cup

The World Mixed Team Championships were initiated in 1989, to be held in conjunction with the World Championships and to provide competition between teams consisting of men and women. The competition was established in memory of Dick Sudirman, father of Indonesian badminton and IBF vice-president. Results to date are as follows: 1989—Indonesia defeated Korea, 3–2.

Can you recall which country has been most successful over the years in winning the Thomas Cup? the Uber Cup? Which countries won these trophies in 1988? Do you know who establishes the badminton rules for play in the United States? By whom is the sport governed for international matches?

The Language of Badminton

Every modern sport has its own particular terminology, and badminton is no exception. Often, these terms seem peculiar to the beginner, but they arise from fascinating origins. Pursuing the origins of the language of individual sports would doubtlessly provide many hours of interesting research.

For example, what explains the "side" of badminton's terms "side-in" and "side-out"? A bit of investigation reveals that in its early years the game was played by sides consisting of at least three players, and usually four or five. Singles and doubles were nonexistent. Instead, a team consisted of several players who served in turn until they were individually eliminated. When all team members had finished serving, thus completing an "inning," that group was said to be "side-out." Currently, the term "service-over" is used in the Laws, but players continue to say "side-out."

The derivations of the terms presented in the following glossary are equally fascinating, and pursuit of them by the curious student would promise interesting results. Some of them have been more fully described in the chapters of this book.

Alley
Extension of the court by 1½ feet on both sides for doubles play.

Anticipation
The art of foreseeing an opponent's next shot.

Back alley
Area between the back boundary line and the long service line for doubles.

Backcourt
The back third of the court, in the area of the back boundary lines.

Backhand
Refers to strokes played on the non-racket side of the body, *i.e.*, with the racket across the body.

Back-swing
Preliminary part of a stroke that carries the racket back in preparation for the forward-swing.

Balk
Any deceptive movement that disconcerts an opponent before or during the service; often called a "feint."

Baseline
Back boundary line at each end of the court, parallel to the net.

Bird

The informal name for badminton's unique object, the shuttlecock; brand names include Bluebird, Eagle, and Parrot!

Block

A stationary stroke, executed by holding the racket in the path of a smashed shuttle, so that it rebounds into the opponent's court.

Carry

An illegal tactic, also called sling or throw, in which the shuttle is caught and held on the racket and then slung during the execution of a stroke.

Center or base position

Location in the center of the court to which a singles player tries to return after each shot.

Center line

Line perpendicular to the net that separates the left and right service courts.

Clear

A shot hit deep to the opponent's back boundary line. The *high clear* is a defensive shot, while the flatter *attacking clear* is used offensively.

Court

Area of play, as defined by the outer boundary lines.

Cross-court

A shot hit diagonally from one side of the court to the other.

Deception

The art of deceiving one's opponent by outright feinting or by disguising a shot's direction and speed until the last moment.

Defense

State of being under attack by the opponent; a style of play consisting mainly of slow drops and high clears.

Double hit

An illegal tactic in which the shuttle is hit twice in succession with two strokes.

Doubles

The game played with two players on each side.

Drive

A fast and low shot that makes a horizontal flight over the net.

Drive serve

A hard, quick serve with a flat trajectory, often used to upset an opponent's pace.

Drop

A shot hit softly and with finesse to fall rapidly and close to the net on the opponent's side.

Ends (of court)

The sections of court on either side of the net, as in "changing ends."

Face

The oval, stringed area of the racket head.

Fault

A violation of the playing rules, either in serving, in receiving, or during play. See Law 14.

First server

In doubles, the player who serves first for a side during a particular inning.

Flat

Describes both the flight of a shuttle with a horizontal trajectory, as well as the angle of the racket face when hitting the shuttle with no "slicing" action.

Flick

A quick wrist and forearm rotation that surprises an opponent by changing an apparently soft shot into a faster passing one; used primarily on the serve and at the net.

Flight

The path or trajectory of the shuttle.

Follow-through

That part of stroke coming after the racket's impact with the shuttle.

Foot fault

A violation of the rules in which the feet of the server or receiver are not in the position required by the Laws.

Footwork

The patterns of foot movement in moving about the court.

Forecourt

The front third of the court, between the net and the short service line.

Forehand

Refers to strokes played on the racket side of the body.

Forward-swing

That part of a stroke carrying the racket forward to the point of contact with the shuttle.

Game

A unit of points necessary for victory: a game consists of fifteen points in men's singles and in all doubles, while eleven points constitutes a game in women's singles. See also "Setting."

Game point

A rally which, if won by the server, ends the game. Also called "game bird."

Grip

The hold on the racket.

Hairpin net shot

A shot made from below and very close to the net with the shuttle rising, just clearing the net, and then dropping sharply down the other side. The shuttle's flight approximates the shape of a hairpin.

Halfcourt shot
A shot hit low and to midcourt, used effectively in doubles against the up-and-back formation.

Hand
An outdated term meaning server, as in "first hand" for "first server."

Head
The end of the racket used for hitting the shuttle, *i.e.*, the strings and the surrounding oval frame.

IBF
International Badminton Federation, the world governing body established in 1934.

Inning
Time during which a player or team holds the service.

In play
The shuttle is "in play" from the time it is struck by the server's racket until it touches the court or a fault or let occurs.

"In" side
The side which holds the serve.

Kill
A fast, downward shot that cannot be returned; a "putaway."

Let
A legitimate cessation of play to allow a rally to be replayed.

Long service line
In singles, the back boundary line; in doubles, a line 2½ feet inside the back boundary line. The serve may not go past this line.

Love
Term for "zero," arising from the English pronunciation of the French word "l'oeuf," meaning "goose-egg" or zero.

Love-all
No score, *i.e.*, zero to zero. To start a match, the umpire calls, "Love-All, Play."

Match
A series of games, usually two out of three, to determine a winner.

Match-point
A rally which, if won by the server, ends the match.

Midcourt
The middle third of the court, halfway between the net and the back boundary line.

Net shot
Shot hit from the forecourt that just clears the net and drops sharply.

No shot
Call made by a player who faults by committing a carry or double hit. Badminton sportsmanship requires that, in the absence of an umpire, players make such calls on themselves.

Obstruction
An illegal tactic in which a player hinders an opponent in the making of a shot.

Offense
State of being on the attack; a style of play consisting mainly of attacking clears, fast drops, and smashes.

Out
Call made by a linesman or player when the shuttle lands outside the boundary lines.

"Out" side
The side which is receiving the serve.

Overhead
Refers to stroke played above head level.

Point
Smallest unit in scoring.

Poona
Early name for badminton in India, coming from a city in which a badminton-like game was played from the 1860s.

Pronation
The inward turning of the wrist and forearm used in all powerful overhead forehand strokes.

Push shot
A gentle shot played by pushing the shuttle with little wrist motion, usually from net or midcourt to the opponent's midcourt.

Racket
The implement used to hit the shuttle.

Rally
An exchange of shots while the shuttle is in play.

Ready position
An alert body position enabling the player to make quick movement in any direction.

Receiver
The player to whom the service is delivered.

Rotation doubles
Rotation of the side-by-side and up-and-back doubles formations.

Round-the-head stroke
An overhead forehand stroke played on the backhand side of the body. The contact point is usually above the opposite shoulder, and a clear, drop, or smash can result.

Rush the serve
Quick move to net in an attempt to put away a low serve by smashing or driving the shuttle out of reach. Used mostly in doubles.

Second server
In doubles, the partner who has second turn at serving for a side during a particular inning.

Serve or service
Stroke used to put the shuttle into play at the start of each rally.

Service court
Area into which the serve must be delivered. This depends on the score and on whether the game is singles or doubles.

Setting
Method of extending a tied game by increasing the number of points necessary to win. Player reaching the tied score first has option of setting.

Set up
A poor shot which makes an easy "kill" for the opponent.

Shaft
The part of the racket between the head and the handle.

Short service line
The line 6½ feet from the net which a serve must reach to be legal.

Shot
The result of a stroke; a shot will be good or bad depending on the execution of the stroke.

Shuttlecock
Official (and ancient) name for shuttle or "bird," badminton's unique projectile.

Sidearm
Refers to stroke played with the arm out to the side of the body.

Side-by-side
A doubles formation.

Side-in and side-out
See the beginning of this section.

Smash
A hard hit overhead shot which forces the shuttle sharply downward. It is badminton's chief attacking stroke.

Stroke
Action of striking the shuttle with the racket.

Supination
The outward turning of the wrist and forearm used on all powerful backhand strokes.

Throat
That part of the racket where the shaft joins the head.

Toss
Before play begins, opponents must toss a coin or spin a racket. The winner may elect to serve, to receive, or to choose an end; the loser has any choice remaining.

USBA

United States Badminton Association. The national governing body for badminton in the United States was founded in 1936 as the American Badminton Association.

Underhand

Refers to stroke that contacts the shuttle below the waist, such as a serve or a clear from the net.

Unsight

In doubles, to stand in such a way that an opponent cannot see the serve being delivered. This is an obstruction and is illegal.

Up-and-back formation

A doubles formation, particularly predominant in mixed doubles.

Wood shot

A shot which results when the base of the shuttle is hit by the frame of the racket. Once illegal, this shot was ruled acceptable by the IBF in 1963.

Do you know the meaning of the following terms: block, game bird, no shot, wood shot?

Laws of Badminton*

(As established by the International Badminton Federation)

With effect from 1st January, 1988

1. Court

1.1   The court shall be a rectangle and laid out as in the following Diagram "A" (except in the case provided for in Law 1.5) and to the measurements there shown, defined by lines 40 mm wide.

1.2   The lines shall be easily distinguishable and preferably be coloured white or yellow.

1.3.1   To show the zone in which a shuttle of correct pace lands when tested (Law 4.4), an additional four marks 40 mm by 40 mm may be made inside each side line for singles of the right service court, 530 mm and 990 mm from the back boundary line.

1.3.2   In making these marks, their width shall be within the measurement given, *i.e.,* the marks will be from 530 mm to 570 mm and from 950 mm to 990 mm from the outside of the back boundary line.

1.4   All lines form part of the area which they define.

1.5   Where space does not permit the marking out of a court for doubles, a court may be marked out for singles only as shown in Diagram "B." The back boundary lines become also the long service lines, and the posts, or the strips of material representing them (Law 2.2), shall be placed on the side lines.

2. Posts

2.1   The posts shall be 1.55 metres in height from the surface of the court. They shall be sufficiently firm to remain vertical and keep the net strained as provided in Law 3, and shall be placed on the doubles side lines as shown in Diagram "A."

2.2   Where it is not practicable to have posts on the side lines, some method must be used to indicate the position of the side lines where they pass under the net, *e.g.,* by the use of thin posts or strips of material 40 mm wide, fixed to the side lines and rising vertically to the net cord.

2.3   On a court marked for doubles, the posts or strips of material representing the posts shall be placed on the side lines for doubles, irrespective of whether singles or doubles is being played.

3. Net

3.1   The net shall be made of fine cord of dark colour and even thickness with a mesh not less than 15 mm and not more than 20 mm.

3.2   The net shall be 760 mm in depth.

*Reprinted with permission of the International Badminton Federation

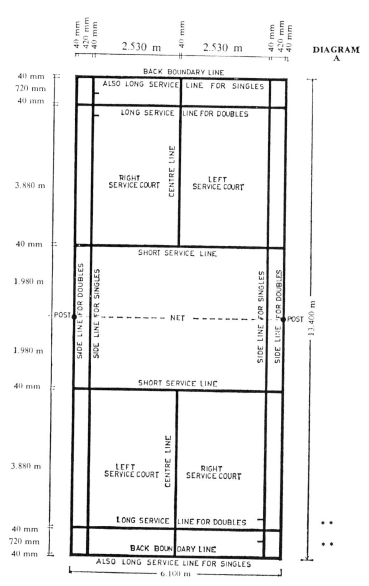

Note: Court which can be used for both
singles and doubles play.

Diagonal length of
full court = 14.723 m

* * Optional testing marks shown opposite

Appendix Figure 1

Note: Court which can be used for both singles and doubles play.

Source: Reprinted with permission of the International Badminton Federation

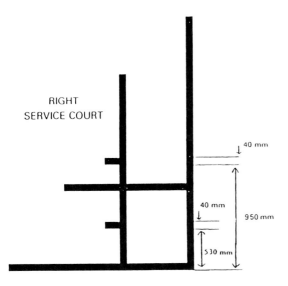

RIGHT
SERVICE COURT

40 mm

40 mm

950 mm

530 mm

N.B. measurement of marks 40 mm by 40 mm

Appendix Figure 2
Optional testing marks for doubles court.
Source: Reprinted with permission of the International Badminton Federation

3.3 The top of the net shall be edged with a 75 mm white tape doubled over a cord or cable running through the tape. This tape must rest upon the cord or cable.

3.4 The cord or cable shall be of sufficient size and weight to be firmly stretched flush with the top of the posts.

3.5 The top of the net from the surface of the court shall be 1.524 metres at the centre of the court and 1.55 metres over the side lines for doubles.

3.6 There shall be no gaps between the ends of the net and the posts. If necessary, the full depth of the net should be tied at the ends.

4. Shuttle

Principles
The shuttle may be made from natural and/or synthetic materials. Whatever material the shuttle is made from, the flight characteristics, generally, should be similar to those produced by a natural feathered shuttle with a cork base covered by a thin layer of leather.
Having regard to the Principles:

4.1 *General Design*
    4.1.1 The shuttle shall have 16 feathers fixed in the base.
    4.1.2 The feathers can have a variable length from 64 mm to 70 mm, but in each shuttle they shall be the same length when measured from the tip to the top of the base.
    4.1.3 The tips of the feathers shall form a circle with a diameter from 58 mm to 68 mm.

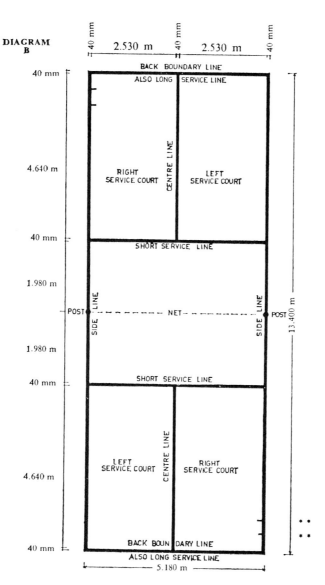

DIAGRAM B

Note: Court which can only be used for singles play.

Diagonal length of singles court = 14.366 m.

* * Optional testing marks shown opposite

Appendix Figure 3
Note: Court which can only be used for singles play.
Source: Reprinted with permission of the International Badminton Federation

Optional Testing Marks for Singles Court
(See Law 1.3)

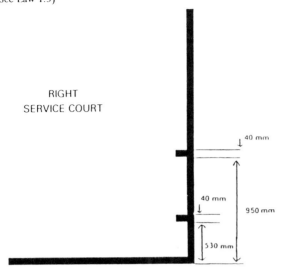

RIGHT
SERVICE COURT

40 mm

40 mm

950 mm

530 mm

N.B. measurement of marks 40 mm by 40 mm

Appendix Figure 4
Optional testing marks for singles court.
Source: Reprinted with permission of the International Badminton Federation

4.1.4   The feathers shall be fastened firmly with thread or other suitable material.

4.1.5   The base shall be:
— 25 mm to 28 mm in diameter
— rounded on the bottom.

4.2   *Weight*
The shuttle shall weigh from 4.74 to 5.50 grams.

4.3   *Non-feathered Shuttle*

4.3.1   The skirt, or simulation of feathers in synthetic materials, replaces natural feathers.

4.3.2   The base is described in Law 4.1.5.

4.3.3   Measurements and weight shall be as in Laws 4.1.2, 4.1.3, and 4.2. However, because of the difference of the specific gravity and behaviour of synthetic materials in comparison with feathers, a variation of up to ten per cent is acceptable.

4.4   *Shuttle Testing*

4.4.1   To test a shuttle, use a full underhand stroke which makes contact with the shuttle over the back boundary line. The shuttle shall be hit at an upward angle and in a direction parallel to the side lines.

4.4.2   A shuttle of correct pace will land not less than 530 mm and not more than 990 mm short of the other back boundary line.

4.5   *Modifications*
Subject to there being no variation in the general design; pace and flight of the shuttle, modifications in the above specifications may be made with the approval of the National Organization concerned:

4.5.1   in places where atmospheric conditions due to either altitude or climate make the standard shuttle unsuitable; or

4.5.2   if special circumstances exist which make it otherwise necessary in the interests of the game.

5. Racket

5.1   The hitting surface of the racket shall be flat and consist of a pattern of crossed strings connected to a frame and either alternately interlaced or bonded where they cross. The stringing pattern shall be generally uniform and, in particular, not less dense in the centre than in any other area.

5.2   The frame of the racket, including the handle, shall not exceed 680 mm in overall length and 230 mm in overall width.

5.3   The overall length of the head shall not exceed 290 mm.

5.4   The strung surface shall not exceed 280 mm in overall length and 220 mm in overall width.

5.5   The racket:

5.5.1   shall be free of attached objects and protrusions, other than those utilised solely and specifically to limit or prevent wear and tear, or vibration, or to distribute weight, or to secure the handle by cord to the player's hand, and which are reasonable in size and placement for such purposes; and

5.5.2   shall be free of any device which makes it possible for a player to change materially the shape of the racket.

6. Approved Equipment

The International Badminton Federation shall rule on any question of whether any racket, shuttle or equipment or any prototypes used in the playing of Badminton complies with the specifications or is otherwise approved or not approved for play. Such ruling may be undertaken on the Federation's initiative or upon application by any party with a bona fide interest therein including any player, equipment manufacturer or National Organization or member thereof.

7. Players

7.1   "Player" applies to all those taking part in a match.

7.2   The game shall be played, in the case of doubles, by two players a side, or in the case of singles, by one player a side.

7.3   The side having the right to serve shall be called the serving side, and the opposing side shall be called the receiving side.

8. Toss

8.1   Before commencing play, the opposing sides shall toss and the side winning the toss shall exercise the choice in either Law 8.1.1 or Law 8.1.2.

8.1.1   To serve or receive first.

8.1.2   To start play at one end of the court or the other.

8.2   The side losing the toss shall then exercise the remaining choice.

9. Scoring

9.1   The opposing sides shall play the best of three games unless otherwise arranged.

9.2   Only the serving side can add a point to its score.

9.3   In doubles and Men's singles a game is won by the first side to score 15 points, except as provided in Law 9.6.

9.4   In Ladies' singles a game is won by the first side to score 11 points, except as provided in Law 9.6.

9.5.1 If the score becomes 13 all or 14 all (9 all or 10 all in Ladies' singles), the side which first scored 13 or 14 (9 or 10) shall have the choice of "setting" or "not setting" the game (Law 9.6).

9.5.2 This choice can only be made when the score is first reached and must be made before the next service is delivered.

9.5.3 The relevant side (Law 9.5.1) is given the opportunity to set at 14 all (10 all in Ladies' singles) despite any previous decision not to set by that side or the opposing side at 13 all (9 all in Ladies' singles).

9.6   If the game has been set, the score is called "Love All" and the side first scoring the set number of points (Law 9.6.1 to 9.6.4) wins the game.

   9.6.1   13 all setting to 5 points
   9.6.2   14 all setting to 3 points
   9.6.3   9 all setting to 3 points
   9.6.4   10 all setting to 2 points

9.7   The side winning a game serves first in the next game.

10. Change of Ends

10.1   Players shall change ends:
   10.1.1   at the end of the first game;
   10.1.2   prior to the beginning of the third game (if any); and
   10.1.3   in the third game, or in a one game match, when the leading score reaches:
      — 6 in a game of 11 points
      — 8 in a game of 15 points

10.2   When players omit to change ends as indicated by Law 10.1, they shall do so immediately the mistake is discovered and the existing score shall stand.

11. Service

11.1   In a correct service:
   11.1.1   neither side shall cause undue delay to the delivery of the service;
   11.1.2   the server and receiver shall stand within diagonally opposite service courts without touching the boundary lines of these service courts; some part of both feet of the server and receiver must remain in contact with the surface of the court in a stationary position until the service is delivered (Law 11.4);
   11.1.3   the server's racket shall initially hit the base of the shuttle while the whole of the shuttle is below the server's waist;
   11.1.4   the shaft of the server's racket at the instant of hitting the shuttle shall be pointing in a downward direction to such an extent that the whole of the head of the racket is discernibly below the whole of the server's hand holding the racket;
   11.1.5   the movement of the server's racket must continue forwards after the start of the service (Law 11.2) until the service is delivered; and
   11.1.6   the flight of the shuttle shall be upwards from the server's racket to pass over the net, so that, if not intercepted, it falls in the receiver's service court.

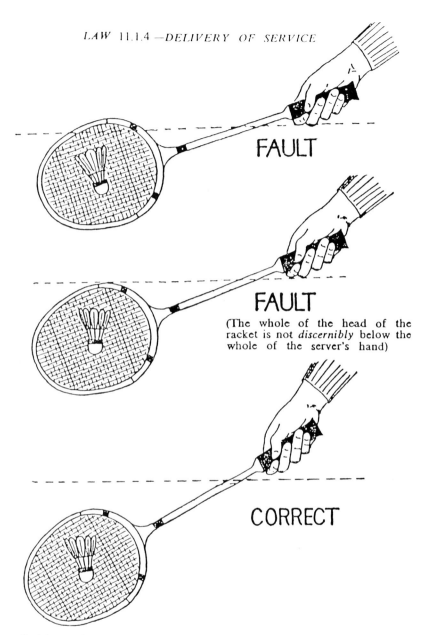

FAULT

FAULT

(The whole of the head of the racket is not *discernibly* below the whole of the server's hand)

CORRECT

Positions of Hand and Racket at the instant of striking the shuttle.

Appendix Figure 5
Illustration of Law 11.1.4—delivery of serve.
Source: Reprinted with permission of the International Badminton Federation

11.2   Once the players have taken their positions, the first forward movement of the server's racket head is the start of the service.

11.3   The server shall not serve before the receiver is ready, but the receiver shall be considered to have been ready if a return of service is attempted.

11.4   The service is delivered when, once started (Law 11.2), the shuttle is hit by the server's racket or the shuttle lands on the floor.

11.5   In doubles, the partners may take up any positions which do not unsight the opposing server or receiver.

12. Singles

12.1   The players shall serve from, and receive in, their respective right service courts when the server has not scored or has scored an even number of points in that game.

12.2   The players shall serve from, and receive in, their respective left service courts when the server has scored an odd number of points in that game.

12.3   If a game is set, the total points scored by the server in that game shall be used to apply Laws 12.1 and 12.2.

12.4   The shuttle is hit alternately by the server and the receiver until a "fault" is made or the shuttle ceases to be in play.

12.5.1   If the receiver makes a "fault" or the shuttle ceases to be in play because it touches the surface of the court inside the receiver's court, the server scores a point. The server then serves again from the alternate service court.

12.5.2   If the server makes a "fault" or the shuttle ceases to be in play because it touches the surface of the court inside the server's court, the server loses the right to continue serving, and the receiver then becomes the server, with no point scored by either player.

13. Doubles

13.1   At the start of a game, and each time a side gains the right to serve, the service shall be delivered from the right service court.

13.2   Only the receiver shall return the service: should the shuttle touch or be hit by the receiver's partner, the serving side scores a point.

13.3.1   After the service is returned, the shuttle is hit by either player of the serving side and then by either player of the receiving side, and so on, until the shuttle ceases to be in play.

13.3.2   After the service is returned, a player may hit the shuttle from any position on that player's side of the net.

13.4.1   If the receiving side makes a "fault" or the shuttle ceases to be in play because it touches the surface of the court inside the receiving side's court, the serving side scores a point, and the server serves again.

13.4.2   If the serving side makes a "fault" or the shuttle ceases to be in play because it touches the surface of the court inside the serving side's court, the server loses the right to continue serving, with no point scored by either side.

13.5.1   The player who serves at the start of any game shall serve from, or receive in, the right service court when that player's side has not scored or has scored an even number of points in that game, and the left service court otherwise.

13.5.2   The player who receives at the start of any game shall receive in, or serve from, the right service court when that player's side has not scored or has scored an even number of points in that game, and the left service court otherwise.

13.5.3   The reverse pattern applies to the partners.

13.5.4   If a game is set, the total points scored by a side in that game shall be used to apply Laws 13.5.1 to 13.5.3.

13.6 Service in any turn of serving shall be delivered from alternate service courts, except as provided in Laws 14 and 16.

13.7 The right to serve passes consecutively from the initial server in any game to the initial receiver in that game, and then consecutively from that player to that player's partner and then to one of the opponents and then the opponent's partner, and so on.

13.8 No player shall serve out of turn, receive out of turn, or receive two consecutive services in the same game, except as provided in Laws 14 and 16.

13.9 Either player of the winning side may serve first in the next game and either player of the losing side may receive.

14. Service Court Errors

14.1 A service court error has been made when a player:
    14.1.1 has served out of turn;
    14.1.2 has served from the wrong service court; or
    14.1.3 standing in the wrong service court, was prepared to receive the service and it has been delivered.

14.2 When a service court error has been made, then:
    14.2.1 if the error is discovered before the next service is delivered, it is a "let" unless only one side was at fault and lost the rally, in which case the error shall not be corrected.
    14.2.2 if the error is not discovered before the next service is delivered, the error shall not be corrected.

14.3 If there is a "let" because of a service court error, the rally is replayed with the error corrected.

14.4 If a service court error is not to be corrected, play in that game shall proceed without changing the players' new service courts (not, when relevant, the new order of serving).

15. Faults

It is a "fault":
15.1 if a service is not correct (Law 11.1);
15.2 if the server, in attempting to serve, misses the shuttle;
15.3 if on service, the shuttle is caught on the net and remains suspended on top or, on service, after passing over the net is caught in the net.
15.4 if in play, the shuttle:
    15.4.1 lands outside the boundaries of the court;
    15.4.2 passes through or under the net;
    15.4.3 fails to pass the net;
    15.4.4 touches the roof, ceiling, or side walls;
    15.4.5 touches the person or dress of a player; or
    15.4.6 touches any other object or person outside the immediate surroundings of the court;
    (*Where necessary on account of the structure of the building, the local badminton authority may, subject to the right of veto of its National Organization, make bye-laws dealing with cases in which a shuttle touches an obstruction.*)
15.5 if, when in play, the initial point of contact with the shuttle is not on the striker's side of the net; (The striker may, however, follow the shuttle over the net with the racket in the course of a stroke.)

15.6 if, when the shuttle is in play, a player:
15.6.1 touches the net or its supports with racket, person, or dress;
15.6.2 invades an opponent's court with racket or person in any degree except as permitted in Law 15.5; or
15.6.3 obstructs an opponent, *i.e.,* prevents an opponent from making a legal stroke where the shuttle is followed over the net;
15.7 if, in play, a player deliberately distracts an opponent by any action such as shouting or making gestures;
15.8 if, in play, the shuttle:
15.8.1 be caught and held on the racket and then slung during the execution of a stroke;
15.8.2 be hit twice in succession by the same player with two strokes; or
15.8.3 be hit by a player and the player's partner successively; or
15.9 if a player is guilty of flagrant, repeated, or persistent offences under Law 18.

16. Lets

"Let" is called by the Umpire, or by a player (if there is no Umpire) to halt play.
16.1 A "let" may be given for any unforeseen or accidental occurrence.
16.2 If a shuttle is caught on the net and remains suspended on top, or after passing over the net is caught in the net, it is a 'let' except during service.
16.3 If during service, the receiver and server are both faulted at the same time, it shall be a "let."
16.4 If the server serves before the receiver is ready it shall be a "let."
16.5 If during play, the shuttle disintegrates and the base completely separates from the rest of the shuttle, it shall be a "let."
16.6 If a Line Judge is unsighted and the Umpire is unable to make a decision, it shall be a "let."
16.7 When a "let" occurs, the play since the last service shall not count, and the player who served shall serve again, except when Law 14 is applicable.

17. Shuttle not in Play

A shuttle is not in play when:
17.1 it strikes the net and remains attached there or suspended on top;
17.2 it strikes the net or post and starts to fall toward the surface of the court on the striker's side of the net;
17.3 it hits the surface of the court; or
17.4 a "fault" or "let" has occurred.

18. Continuous Play, Misconduct, Penalties

18.1 Play shall be continuous from the first service until the match is concluded, except as allowed in Laws 18.2 and 18.3.
18.2 An interval not exceeding 5 minutes is allowed between the second and third games of all matches in all of the following situations:
18.2.1 in international competitive events;
18.2.2 in IBF sanctioned events; and
18.2.3 in all other matches (unless the National Organization has previously published a decision not to allow such an interval).

18.3 When necessitated by circumstances not within the control of the players, the Umpire may suspend play for such a period as the Umpire may consider necessary. If play be suspended, the existing score shall stand and play be resumed from that point.

18.4 Under no circumstances shall play be suspended to enable a player to recover his strength or wind, or to receive instruction or advice.

18.5.1 Except in the intervals provided in Laws 18.2 and 18.3, no player shall be permitted to receive advice during a match.

18.5.2 Except at the conclusion of a match, no player shall leave the court without the Umpire's consent.

18.6 The Umpire shall be the sole judge of any suspension of play.

18.7 A player shall not:

18.7.1 deliberately cause suspension of play;

18.7.2 deliberately interfere with the speed of the shuttle;

18.7.3 behave in an offensive manner; or

18.7.4 be guilty of misconduct not otherwise covered by the Laws of Badminton.

18.8 The Umpire shall administer any breach of Law 18.4, 18.5 or 18.7 by:

18.8.1 issuing a warning to the offending side;

18.8.2 faulting the offending side, if previously warned; or

18.8.3 in cases of flagrant offence or persistent offences, faulting the offending side and reporting the offending side immediately to the Referee, who shall have the power to disqualify.

18.9 Where a Referee has not been appointed, the responsible official shall have the power to disqualify.

19. Officials and Appeals

19.1 The Referee is in overall charge of the tournament or event of which a match forms part.

19.2 The Umpire, where appointed, is in charge of the match, the court, and its immediate surrounds. The Umpire shall report to the Referee. In the absence of a Referee, the Umpire shall report instead to the responsible official.

19.3 The Service Judge shall call service faults made by the server should they occur (Law 11).

19.4 A Line Judge shall indicate whether a shuttle is "in" or "out."

An Umpire shall:

19.5 uphold and enforce the Laws of Badminton and, especially call a "fault" or "let" should either occur, without appeal being made by the players;

19.6 give a decision on any appeal regarding a point of dispute, if made before the next service is delivered;

19.7 ensure players and spectators are kept informed of the progress of the match;

19.8 appoint or remove Line Judges or a Service Judge in consultation with the Referee;

19.9 not overrule the decisions of Line Judges and the Service Judge on points of fact;

19.10.1 where another court official is not appointed, arrange for their duties to be carried out;

19.10.2 where an appointed official is unsighted, carry out the official's duties or play a "let";

19.11 decide upon any suspension of play;

19.12 record and report to the Referee all matters in relation to Law 18; and

19.13 take to the Referee all unsatisfied appeals on questions of Law only.
(Such appeals must be made before the next service is delivered, or, if at the end of a game, before the side that appeals has left the court.)

Appendices to the Laws of Badminton

Imperial Measurements

The Laws express all measurements in metres or millimetres. Imperial measurements are acceptable and for the purposes of the Laws the following table of equivalence should be used:

15 millimetres	⅝ inch
20 millimetres	¾ inch
25 millimetres	1 inch
28 millimetres	1⅛ inches
40 millimetres	1½ inches
58 millimetres	2¼ inches
64 millimetres	2½ inches
68 millimetres	2⅝ inches
70 millimetres	2¾ inches
75 millimetres	3 inches
220 millimetres	8⅝ inches
230 millimetres	9 inches
280 millimetres	11 inches
290 millimetres	11⅜ inches
380 millimetres	1 foot 3 inches
420 millimetres	1 foot 4½ inches
490 millimetres	1 foot 7½ inches
530 millimetres	1 foot 9 inches
570 millimetres	1 foot 10½ inches
680 millimetres	2 feet 2¾ inches
720 millimetres	2 feet 4½ inches
760 millimetres	2 feet 6 inches
950 millimetres	3 feet 1½ inches
990 millimetres	3 feet 3 inches
1.524 metres	5 feet
1.55 metres	5 feet 1 inch
2.53 metres	8 feet 3¾ inches
3.88 metres	12 feet 9 inches
4.64 metres	15 feet 3 inches
5.18 metres	17 feet
6.1 metres	20 feet
13.4 metres	44 feet

Handicap Matches

In handicap matches, the following variations in the Laws apply:

1. "Setting" is not permitted (*i.e.,* Laws 9.5 and 9.6 do not apply).
2. Law 10.1.3 will be amended to read:
   "In the third game, and in a one game match, when one side has scored half the total number of points required to win the game (the next higher number being taken in case of fractions)."

Games of Other Than 11 or 15 Points

It is permissible to play one game of 21 points by prior arrangement. In this case the following variations in Laws 9.3, 9.5.1, 9.5.3, and 9.6 apply:
Replace "13", "14" and "15" by "19", "20" and "21" respectively.
To Law 10.1.3 shall be added "—11 in a game of 21 points."

Vocabulary

This list is the standard vocabulary that should be used by Umpires to control a match.

1. *Announcements and Introductions*
   - 1.1   "Ladies and Gentlemen," this is:
     - 1.1.1   the semi-final, or final, of Men's Singles, etc., or
     - 1.1.2   the first singles of the Thomas Cup (Uber Cup) tie between .... (Country) and .... (Country)
   - 1.2   On my right ....(Country) represented by ....(name)

     On my left .... (Country) represented by ....(name)
   - 1.3   .... to serve .... to receive.

2. *Start of Match and Calling the Score*
   - 2.1   "Love-all; play"
   - 2.2   "Service Over"
   - 2.3   "Second Server"
   - 2.4   "..................................... Game Point ...." *e.g.,* "14 game point 6"
   - 2.5   "..................................... Match Point ...." *e.g.,* "14 match point 8"
   - 2.6   "..................................... Game Point ...." *e.g.,* "2 game point all"
   - 2.7   "Game won by ....(and the score) ...."
   - 2.8   "Second game won by ....(and the score) ...."
   - 2.9   "Are you setting?"
     - 2.9.1   "Setting 2 points; Love-all"
     - 2.9.2   "Setting 3 points; Love-all"
     - 2.9.3   "Setting 5 points; Love-all"
   - 2.10   "Game not set" (Call score "9-all, play"; "13-all, play," etc.)
   - 2.11   "One game all"
   - 2.12   "Court .... a five-minute interval has been claimed"
   - 2.13.1   "Court ....two minutes remaining"
   - 2.13.2   "Court ....one minute remaining"

3. *General Communication*
   - 3.1   "Are you ready?"
   - 3.2   "Come here please"
   - 3.3   "Is the shuttle O.K.?"
   - 3.4   "Test the shuttle" (only for wobble, NOT speed)
   - 3.5   "Change the shuttle"
   - 3.6   "Do NOT change the shuttle"
   - 3.7   "Play a 'let' "
   - 3.8   "Change ends, please"
   - 3.9   "You served out of turn"
   - 3.10   "You received out of turn"
   - 3.11   "You must not interfere with the speed of the shuttle"
   - 3.12   "The shuttle touched you"
   - 3.13   "You touched the net"
   - 3.14   "You are standing in the wrong court"
   - 3.15   "You invaded your opponent's court"
   - 3.16   "You obstructed your opponent"
   - 3.17   "Fault—receiver"
   - 3.18   "Service fault called"
   - 3.19   "Play must be continuous"
   - 3.20   "Play is suspended"
   - 3.21   .... (name of player) "Warning for misconduct"
   - 3.22   .... (name of player) "Fault for misconduct"
   - 3.23   "Fault"

3.24   "Out"

3.25   "Line Judge—signal please"

3.26   "Service Judge—signal please"

3.27   "First server"

3.28   "Wipe the court"

4. *End of Match*

4.1   "Match won by ...." (In team event, use name of country.)

5. *Scoring*

0—Love	10—Ten
1—One	11—Eleven
2—Two	12—Twelve
3—Three	13—Thirteen
4—Four	14—Fourteen
5—Five	15—Fifteen
6—Six	16—Sixteen
7—Seven	17—Seventeen
8—Eight	18—Eighteen
9—Nine	

Badminton for Disabled People

The following amended Laws of Badminton are applicable to the various categories of disabled people as listed:

(a) AMBULANT (no change in the Laws)

Persons requiring no mechanical aid to perambulation.

(b) SEMI-AMBULANT

Persons capable of erect perambulation but only with mechanical aid such as:—

crutch(es)

stick(s)

support frame

leg brace(s)

artificial leg(s)

(c) NON-AMBULANT

Persons whose disabilities dictate that they adopt a sedentary posture using such support as:—

chair

wheel-chair

stool

The table below shows the changes to Laws.

LAW	SEMI-AMBULANT	NON-AMBULANT
11.1.3 and 11.1.4	No Change	As some medical conditions which render a player "Non-Ambulant" may also positively preclude compliance, these Laws to be deleted in entirety.

11.1.2   The wording of this Law to be extended so as to require every part of the server's and receiver's "mechanical aid" or "support" that is in contact with the surface of the court also to be within the appropriate service court and in a stationary position until the service is delivered. The word "diagonally" to be deleted.

12.   *Singles Play*

Shaded area indicates extent of court.

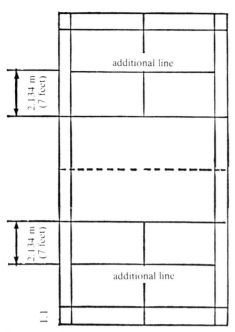

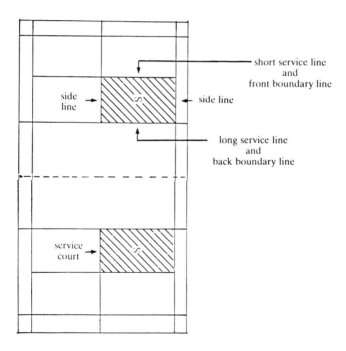

As only ONE service court exists at each end, references to 'Left' and 'Right' and 'alternate service court' do not apply.

13.   *Doubles Play*
       Shaded area indicates extent of court.

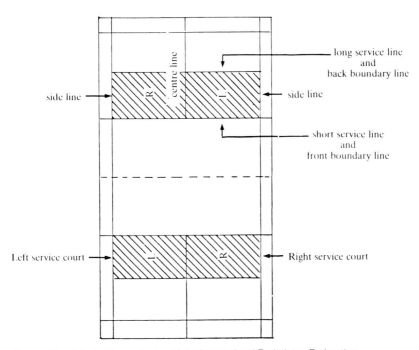

Source: Reprinted with permission of the International Badminton Federation

Players must serve from and receive within the same service courts, as adopted at the beginning of a game, throughout that game.

When the service is not returned or a "fault" is made by the receiving side, and the serving side thereby scores a point:

the service passes to the other player of the serving side and is delivered from the other service court and continues to alternate thus as long as the serving side continues to score.

15.4.5   The wording of this Law to be extended so as to make it a "fault" if the player or his "mechanical aid" or "support" touches the shuttle.

All Other Laws

To remain unchanged for all classifications. (This includes Law 4 with the pace of the shuttle being measured against the length of a standard court by an able-bodied or ambulant player. A shuttle passing this test is suitable for play by all.)

References

General Books about Badminton

Adams, Bernard. *The Badminton Story.*
London: British Broadcasting
Publications, 1980.

Davis, Pat. *Guinness Book of Badminton.*
London: Guinness Superlatives Ltd.,
1983. (Order from Sterling)

Hales, Diane. A History of Badminton in the
United States from 1878–1939. Masters
thesis, California Polytechnic University,
Pomona, CA. Interlibrary loan. June,
1979.

Books for Players and Coaches

Annarino, Anthony A. *Badminton
Instruction Program.* Englewood Cliffs,
NJ: Prentice-Hall, 1973.

Badminton Association of England (ed.).
Know the Game—Badminton. London:
E. P. Publishing Co., Ltd., 1950, 12th
edition 1976. (Order from Sportshelf)

Ballou, Ralph. *Teaching Badminton* (Sports
Teaching Series). New York: Burgess,
1982.

Brown, Edward. *The Complete Book of
Badminton.* Harrisburg, PA: Stackpole
Books, 1969.

Burris, Barbara and Olson, Arne. *Badminton*
(Sports-Techniques Series). Chicago:
Athletic Institute (805 Merchandise Mart
Plaza), 1970.

Crossley, Ken G. *Progressive Badminton.*
London: Bell Publishers, rev. 1980. (Order
from Sportshelf)

Davidson, Kenneth R. and Gustavson,
Lealand R. *Winning Badminton.* New
York: A. S. Barnes and Company, 1953.
Melbourne (FL): Krieger Publishing Co.,
rev. 1964.

Davis, Pat. *The Badminton Coach: A
Manual for Coaches, Teachers, and
Players.* New Rochelle, NY: Sportshelf,
1976.

————. *Badminton Complete.* London: Kaye
and Ward, 1967, rev. 1982.

————. *Badminton, The Complete Practical
Guide.* London: David and Charles, 1982.

Devlin, Frank and Lardner, Rex. *Sports
Illustrated Book of Badminton.*
Harcourt-Row, 1973.

Downey, Jake. *Badminton for Schools.*
London: Pelham Books, 1978.

————. *Better Badminton for All.* London:
Kaye and Ward, 1975. (Order from
Merrimack Publ. Cir.)

————. *Winning Badminton Singles.*
London: E. P. Publishing Co., 1983.
(Order from Sterling)

————. *Winning Badminton Doubles.*
London: Adam and Charles Black, 1984.

Finston, Irv and Remsberg, Charles. *Inside
Badminton.* Chicago: Contemporary
Books, Inc., 1979.

Grice, Tony. *Badminton.* American Press,
1981.

Hashman, Judy Devlin. *Winning Badminton.*
London: Ward Lock, 1984.

Hicks, Virginia. *The How to of Badminton
From Player to Teacher.* Denton, TX:
Terrell Wheeler Printing, Inc., 1973.

Johnson, M. L. *Badminton.* Philadelphia:
W. B. Saunders Co., 1974.

Johnson, M. L. and Johnson, Dewayne.
Badminton. American Press, 1981.

Krotee, March L. and Turner, Edward.
*Innovative Theory and Practice of
Badminton.* Kendall-Hunt, 1984.

Mills, R. J. *Badminton.* London: E. P.
Publishing, Ltd., 1975. (Order from
Charles River Books)

Moore, Ballard J. and Henderson, Thomas E.
Shuttlecock Action. Kendall-Hunt, 1977.

Paup, Donald C. and Breen, James L. *Winning Badminton*. Chicago: Athletic Institute, 1984.

Poole, James. *Badminton* (Goodyear Physical Activities Series). Glenview, IL: Scott, Foresman and Company, 1982.

Reznik, Jack and Byrd, Ron. *Badminton*. Gorsuch-Scarisbrick, 1987.

Rogers, T. Wynn. *Advanced Badminton* (Physical Education Activities Series). Dubuque, IA: Wm. C. Brown Company Publishers, 1970.

Roper, Peter. *Badminton: The Skills of the Game*. London: Crowood Press, 1985. (Order from Longwood Publishing Group)

Squires, Dick. *The Other Racket Sports*, Ch. 6, pp. 91–115. New York: McGraw-Hill Book Co., 1978.

Sullivan, George. *Guide to Badminton*. New York: Fleet Press Corp., 1968.

Talbot, Derek. *Badminton to the Top*. Wakefield (England): EP Publishing Limited, 1981. (Order from Sterling)

Watson, Alex. *Winning Badminton*. Toronto: Coles Publishing Co., 1976. (same as Mills, above)

Whetnall, Paul and Leahy, Trevor. *Badminton* (Competitive Sports Services). Batsford, England, 1987. (Order from David and Charles)

Wright, Les. *Your Book of Badminton*. London: Faber and Faber Publishers, 1972. (Order from Transatlantic)

Significant Earlier Books

(now out of print, but often available in libraries)

Choong, E. and Brundle, F. *Badminton*. New York: Dover Publications, 1953.

———. *The Phoenix Book of Badminton*. London: Phoenix House, 1956; New York: The Philosophical Library.

Davidson, Kenneth R. and Smith, Lenore C. *Badminton* (Athletic Institute Series). New York: Sterling Publishing Co., Inc., 1961.

Devlin, J. Frank. *Badminton for All*. Garden City, NY: Doubleday, Doran and Company, Inc., 1937.

Friedrich, John and Rutledge, Abbie. *Beginning Badminton*. Belmont (CA): Wadsworth Publishing Co., Inc., 1962.

Hashman, Judy Devlin. *A Champion's Way*. London: Kaye and Ward, 1969.

Thomas, Sir George. *The Art of Badminton*. London: Hutchinson, 1923.

Teaching and Coaching Guides

Badminton-Squash-Racquetball Guide. NAGWS-AAHPER, 1201 16th Street NW, Washington D.C. 20036. (Once known as *Tennis Badminton Guide*.)

First Coaching Seminar, Peking, China, March 26–April 2, 1977. Asian Badminton Confederation, 101 Cecil Street #16-01, Tong Eng Building, Singapore 0106.

Manuals for Instructing, Coaching, and Training. Canadian Badminton Association, 333 River Road, Toronto, Ontario, Canada K1L 8H9.

Selected Tennis and Badminton Articles. NAGWS-AAHPER, 1201 16th Street NW, Washington D.C. 20036.

Your Guide to Better Badminton. Ashaway Line and Twine Company. Ashaway, Rhode Island 02804.

Rules Books

C.B.A. Handbook. Canadian Badminton Association, 333 River Road, Toronto, Ontario, Canada K1L 8H9.

I.B.F. Statute Book. The International Badminton Federation, 24 Winchcombe House, Winchcombe Street, Cheltenham, Gloucestershire, England GL52 2NA.

Official Rules of Play (U.S.B.A. Handbook). United States Badminton Association, 501 W. Sixth St., Papillion, NE 68046.

Magazines

Asian Badminton. Asian Badminton Confederation, 101 Cecil Street #16-01, Tong Eng Building, Singapore 0106.

Badminton Canada. Canadian Badminton Association, 333 River Road, Ottawa, Ontario, Canada K1L 8H9.

The Badminton Magazine. P.O. Box 3796, Manhattan Beach, CA 90266.

Badminton Now. The Badminton Association of England, National Badminton Centre, Bradwell Road, Loughton Lodge, Milton Keynes MK8 9LA, England.

Badminton U.S.A. United States Badminton Association, 501 W. Sixth St., Papillion, NE 68046.

Racquets Canada. Raxport Publishing Ltd., 22A Cumberland Street, Suite 202, Toronto, Ontario M4W IJ5, Canada.

World Badminton. The International Badminton Federation, 24 Winchcombe House, Winchcombe Street, Cheltenham, Gloucestershire, England GL52 2NA.

Films and Videos

Advanced Badminton. Wynn Rogers, Aims Instructional Media Services, Inc., P.O. Box 1010, Hollywood, CA 90028.

Badminton Fundamentals. Aims Instructional Media Services, Inc., P.O. Box 1010, Hollywood, CA 90028.

Badminton Movies. Louisville Badminton Supply, 9411 Westport Road, Louisville, KY 40222.

Badminton Sound Films. AAHPER Educational Media Services, 1201 16th Street NW, Washington D.C. 20036.

Badminton Sound Super 8 Cassettes. 1974. AAHPER Educational Media Services, 1201 16th Street NW, Washington D.C. 20036.

C.B.A. Video Library. Canadian Badminton Association, 333 River Road, Toronto, Ontario M4W 1J5, Canada.

Selected Highlights of the 1973 U.S. Open Amateur Championships. Travelers Insurance Companies, 1 Tower Square, Hartford, CT 06115.

U.S.B.A. Video Library (20 videocassettes of national and international events). United States Badminton Association, 501 W. Sixth St., Papillion, NE 68046.

Questions and Answers

True or False

1. The thumb is placed flat against the back bevel of the handle for the fore-hand grip. (pp. 24–25)
2. The racket is held tightly in the palm of the hand. (p. 25)
3. Backpedaling, the skill of moving backwards, is peculiar to the game of badminton. (p. 30)
4. A legal serve requires that both the contact point and racket head be below the wrist. (pp. 15, 31)
5. The serve is considered a defensive stroke because it is played underhand and must therefore be hit upwards. (p. 34)
6. All forehand strokes originate high above the head with the wrist cocked. (p. 45)
7. The trajectory of the attacking clear is lower than the defensive clear. (p. 36)
8. The dropshot should be deceptive since its flight is slow. (p. 40)
9. A smash played from the backcourt will have less downward angle than one played nearer the net. (p. 42)
10. With proper timing it is not necessary to use shoulder and arm strength to obtain power. (p. 41)
11. A drive may be played deep and fast or slower to midcourt, as well as cross-court and down-the-line. (p. 47)
12. The backhand clear is one of the easiest strokes to play and perfect. (p. 75)
13. The half-smash has little value since it has less speed than a full smash. (p. 44)
14. The round-the-head shot is a forehand shot played above the left shoulder. (pp. 73–74)
15. The drive serve is designed to push the receiver to the backcourt. (pp. 47–48)
16. Net shots are played with the same wrist and shoulder action as other shots. (pp. 48–49)
17. Underhand shots are normally considered offensive shots. (p. 34)
18. "Holding the shuttle" is a useful deceptive technique, especially against a fast-moving player. (p. 80)
19. Repeated practice of each stroke separately tends to make a player lose the sense of game play. (p. 65)

20. Practicing or playing with a player of like ability produces maximum benefits. (p. 65)
21. Defensive play can be changed to offensive play depending on how well a stroke is executed and selected for use at the time. (p. 53)
22. Angle of return in badminton is relatively unimportant since the court is only twenty feet wide. (p. 54)
23. Crosscourt shots are best used when your opponent has not been drawn from the center position. (p. 55)
24. Receiving serve in a diagonal (forward and back) stance allows the receiver to cover best the area to either side of him. (p. 55)
25. In singles, the object is to move your opponent forward and back using low serves, drives, and dropshots. (pp. 56–57)
26. The half-smash and dropshot are often used to change defense into attack. (p. 61)
27. A short clear should be returned with a smash or dropshot. (p. 57)
28. In singles, the forehand side of the court may be vulnerable due to extra effort made compensating for weakness on the backhand. (p. 66)
29. In doubles, teams should decide to play side-by-side or up-and-back without changing this formation during a point. (pp. 58–61)
30. Offense and defense are determined by the angle of the flight of the shuttle. (p. 53)
31. The side-by-side formation lends itself best to attack. (pp. 58–59)
32. The up-and-back formation is best attacked with half-court shots. (pp. 59–60)
33. A high deep clear allows a team to assume the up-and-back positions. (p. 61)
34. A well played half-court shot should lead each opponent to believe it is his shot to return. (p. 60)
35. In mixed doubles, the woman should seldom make an attempt to return smashes and fast drives. (p. 63)
36. Except when there is a set-up, the net player in doubles uses many halfcourt and net shots. (p. 63)
37. There is a special formation to use in mixed doubles when the opposing man plays an overhead smash. (p. 64)
38. The woman in mixed doubles should often play the shuttle deep to the corners. (p. 63)
39. In mixed doubles, the man should attempt to play most of the shots and direct them to the opposing woman. (p. 63)
40. A balk is a deceptive and delaying movement used legally as a means of gaining a point. (p. 16)
41. A carry is legal provided the flight of the shuttle is not drastically altered. (p. 17)
42. A flick shot refers to shots played with an overhead stroke to surprise an opponent. (p. 81)
43. A shuttle becomes "in play" the moment the serve crosses the net. (p. 12)
44. The serving side wins the point when a let is called. (p. 12)

45. The term "second server" means the team which did not serve first in the game. (p. 14)
46. When setting, the player reaching the tied score first has the option of setting. (p. 12)
47. A shot played off the frame of the racket is legal. (p. 17)
48. The heavier the shuttle, the faster it flies. (p. 9)
49. A player losing the toss has no choices. (p. 11)
50. In the third game of a doubles match, players change ends when one team scores eight points. (p. 12)
51. A doubles team may not change its order of service during the match. (pp. 13–15)
52. It is considered poor sportsmanship to change the speed of the shuttle by bending the feathers without the opponent's agreement. (p. 18)
53. A shuttlecock will have a slower flight at a high altitude and with low humidity. (p. 9)
54. Tournaments are played both indoors and outdoors. (p. 9)

Completion

55. Identify the names of the following lines and areas of a badminton court.
    1. _____
    2. _____
    3. _____
    4. _____
    5. _____
    6. _____
    7. _____
    8. _____
    9. _____
    10. _____ (pp. 4–5)

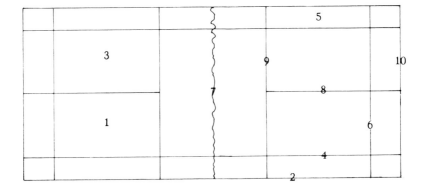

56. Net heights _____ (p. 3)
57. Shuttle weights _____ (p. 7)
58. Minimum ceiling height _____ (p. 3)

Give the required number of points for:

59. Women's singles _____ (pp. 3, 12)
60. Men's singles _____ (pp. 3, 12)
61. Doubles _____ (pp. 3, 12)
62. Score set at 9 all _____ (pp. 3, 12)
63. Score set at 10 all _____ (pp. 3, 12)
64. Score set at 13 all _____ (pp. 3, 12)
65. Score set at 14 all _____ (pp. 3, 12)
66. On the court below draw and number the flight patterns for the following strokes:
    1. Defensive Clear
    2. Attacking Clear
    3. Overhead Dropshot
    4. Smash
    5. High Singles Serve
    6. Low Doubles Serve
    7. High Doubles Serve
    8. Drive
    9. Hairpin Net Shot
    10. Underhand Clear

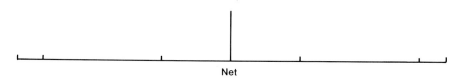

Net

Multiple Choice

Select one of the following letters to best answer the question.

A. point scored	E. second server
B. service over	F. legal
C. let	G. disqualification
D. fault	H. poor etiquette

67. A player attempting a serve, misses the shuttle completely. (p. 16)
68. A smash played by the server hits the outside edge of the line. (p. 12)
69. After the serve a player inadvertently places one foot outside the boundary lines to play the shuttle. (p. 15)
70. In singles, the server's score is seven and he serves from the right court and wins the rally. (p. 16)

71. Neither the linesman nor the umpire can make a decision when the serving side served a shuttle which fell very close to the short service line. (p. 19)
72. The server contacts the shuttle below the waist and the racket head below the hand. (p. 15)
73. The server in singles takes a step during the stroke but before the shuttle is contacted. (p. 15)
74. The receiver unsuccessfully returns a serve he claims was served before he was ready. (p. 15)
75. In doubles, the receiver receives serve in the wrong court and wins the rally. (p. 16)
76. In doubles, a player receives serve twice in succession and the serving side wins both rallies. (p. 16)
77. The receiver's partner is able to return a serve his partner cannot reach and scores a winner. (p. 16)
78. The shuttle passes between the net and net post and falls into the proper court. (p. 16)
79. A player contacts the shuttle on his side but the racket head carries over the net. (p. 16)
80. A player touches the net on the follow-through of a smash after the shuttle hit the floor. (p. 16)
81. The server hits an opponent with a shuttle which is going out. (p. 17)
82. The net player is able to return a net smash by ducking below the net and putting his racket up in front of the shuttle. (p. 17)
83. In mixed doubles, the server places himself behind his partner in order to hide the shuttle from the receiver. (p. 17)
84. A player consults his coach between the first and second games. (p. 17)
85. A player calls no shot or fault whenever it occurs during play. (p. 18)
86. In doubles, with the score 8–7, the first server serves and the serve hits the top of the net and lands in the correct court. (p. 16)

Question Answer Key
True or False

1. F	12. F	23. F	34. T	45. F
2. F	13. F	24. F	35. T	46. T
3. F	14. T	25. F	36. T	47. T
4. T	15. F	26. T	37. T	48. T
5. T	16. F	27. T	38. F	49. F
6. F	17. F	28. T	39. F	50. T
7. T	18. T	29. F	40. F	51. F
8. T	19. F	30. T	41. F	52. T
9. T	20. T	31. F	42. F	53. F
10. F	21. T	32. T	43. F	54. F
11. T	22. F	33. F	44. F	

Completion

55. 1. Right Service Court
    2. Side Boundary Line (doubles)
    3. Left Service Court
    4. Side Boundary Line (singles)
    5. Alley
    6. Long Service Line for Doubles
    7. Net
    8. Center Line
    9. Short Service Line
    10. Back Boundary Line and Long Service Line for Singles
56. 5' center, 5'1'' posts
57. 4.74–5.50 grams
58. 30' above entire court
59. 11 points
60. 15 points
61. 15 points
62. 3 points
63. 2 points
64. 5 points
65. 3 points
66.

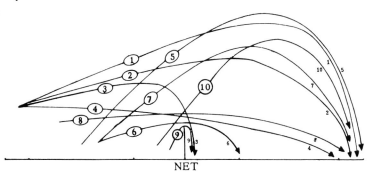

NET

Multiple Choice

67. D	77. A or D
68. A	78. D
69. F	79. F
70. C	80. F
71. C	81. A
72. F	82. D
73. B or D	83. D
74. A	84. D or G
75. C	85. H
76. A	86. A or F

index